HERTFORDSHIRE LIBRARY SERVICE

RENEWAL
INFORM-
ATION

L.32A

This book is due for return on or before the date shown. You may extend its loan by bringing the book to the library or, once only, by post or telephone, quoting the date of return, the letter and number on the date card, if applicable, and the information at the top of this label.

The loan of books in demand cannot be extended.

Please renew/return this item by the last date shown.

So that your telephone call is charged at local rate, please call the numbers as set out below:

	From Area codes 01923 or 0208:	From the rest of Herts:
Renewals:	01923 471373	01438 737373
Enquiries:	01923 471333	01438 737333
Minicom:	01923 471599	01438 737599

L32b

THE EAST RIDING

THE EAST RIDING

GEOFFREY N. WRIGHT

B. T. Batsford Ltd
London

First published 1976
Copyright © Geoffrey N. Wright 1976
Printed in Great Britain by Biddles of Guildford
for the publishers B. T. Batsford Ltd
4 Fitzhardinge Street, London W1A 0AH

ISBN 0 7134 3102 4

CONTENTS

ACKNOWLEDGEMENT

The photographs in this book are all by the author with the exception of no. 4 which is by A. F. Kersting, F.R.P.S.

ILLUSTRATIONS

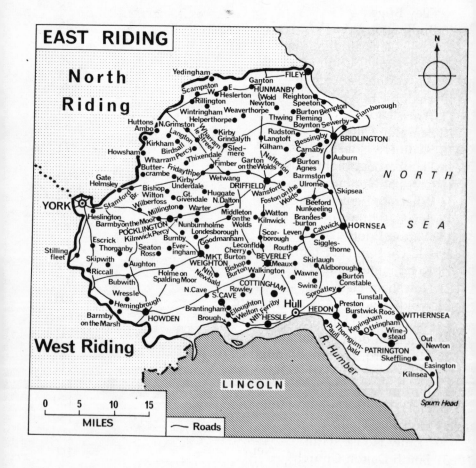

Map of East Riding

CHAPTER ONE

Introduction

The East Riding is the smallest of Yorkshire's three Ridings. It is also the least populated, the least known, the most rural, and the longest settled. Lacking the stern Pennine heights of its western sister, it has equally little in common with the North Riding's moors and dales, and its coastline is vastly different from that to the north of Scarborough. At its highest, the East Riding just manages to top 800 feet at Garrowby Hill; it is wold and vale country of the gentle contours characteristic of chalk and clay, of dry uplands and sluggish, winding rivers. It has also a changing, vanishing coastline extending from Filey Brigg to Spurn Head. Although York itself is shared by all the Ridings, for our purposes we are including it in this book, making it a splendid gateway to the quieter delights beyond.

In shape, the East Riding is rather like a partly-opened fan radiating from Spurn Head. One edge lies along the Humber and Ouse making a southern boundary like a flattened 'S'. Open the fan to a third of its span, and its other edge becomes the coastal boundary of the Riding. The convex leaves of the fan's working edge represent the course of the Derwent, for much of its journey the boundary between East and North Ridings.

In geological terms the rocks of Yorkshire dip from west to east, the oldest and highest in the Pennines, the lowest and most recent deposits in Holderness, by the coast, each layer overlapping its older neighbour. The Vale of York, which includes the Derwent valley, has a base of red sandstone of Triassic times overlaid by fertile alluvial deposits, clays generally along the Derwent valley, sands between it and the Ouse and towards the Wolds. In both there is a high water-table, so that drainage, especially in the clayey soils, has always been a problem. The efficiency with which the problem has been solved has dictated the use of the land, that which is constantly liable to flooding usually being under permanent grass.

Eastwards from the Vale of York is the great chalk mass of the Wolds forming a crescent from Flamborough to North Ferriby. Highest and broadest near the centre of the crescent these Yorkshire Wolds are chalk, not limestone, giving gentle, rolling scenery which is never spectacular, except at the coastal cliffs. There are many branching dry valleys, but few natural rock outcrops, although the Wolds do present a steep scarp-face towards the Vale of Pickering in the north and the Vale of York in the west, from which they are separated by a narrow bench of Jurassic rock. A number of villages are sited along this strip, attracted by the presence of springs at the foot of the chalk, and the good building qualities of the sandstones and limestones.

The chalk dips eastwards to merge with the peaty deposits on the alluvial floor of the valley of the River Hull. Their dark soils are easily distinguished on the ground, their positions identified on the map by the frequent use of the word 'carrs', lands liable to seasonal flooding. Between the Hull valley and the coast is the drift landscape of Holderness, a thick deposit of boulder-clay and other glacial materials which overlay the chalk base. Nowhere does the land here exceed 75 feet above sea level; in some places the soil is a clay-loam, but there are sandy, gravelly patches giving lighter soils which helped to create the old distinction between 'wheat' or 'turnip' land.

South of Bridlington, the East Riding coastline extends for 40 miles to Spurn Head, the longest stretch of boulder-clay coast in Britain. Rarely exceeding 40 feet high, the red or purple cliffs are being eroded more rapidly than any other part of our coast, two yards a year. The Ice Age created this coast 25,000 years ago; the North Sea is taking it away, and at the same time is adding to the periodic growth of Spurn Head. Westwards along the Humber from Spurn's beckoning finger, the tides and the estuary have been man's allies in reclaiming many square miles of rich farmland, so that the old town of Hedon, a flourishing port in the Middle Ages, is now two miles inland.

Against this physical background man's story covers perhaps 5,000 years. The porous soils and light tree cover of the chalk Wolds attracted the earliest settlers of Neolithic times, whose longbarrows are dispersed across the Wolds from Market Weighton to Folkton, near Filey. Particularly impressive burials in such barrows have been excavated at Hanging Grimston and on Willerby Wold. At Duggleby Howe is one of the largest round barrows, of late Neolithic period (1800 B.C.). Probably contemporary with Stonehenge, the East Riding claims England's tallest single standing stone at Rudston.

Evidence of Iron Age occupation comes from the great barrow cemetery of Danes' Graves, three miles north of Driffield; and near Flamborough the defensive earthwork called Danes Dyke cuts across the headland, on a north-south line two and a half miles long. Dating from 200–100 B.C. it is one of a number of linear earthworks of similar period farther inland on the eastern slopes of the Wolds.

In A.D. 71 the Romans established a permanent fortress at York designed to house a legion of 6,000 men. Roman occupation had its greatest influence in the towns; the native population would have been little affected, their closest contact being through the occasional visits of the Roman tax collectors. The Romans established a ferry across the Humber making an alternative route from Lincoln to York via Stamford Bridge, and created another route northwards to Malton. Along the Yorkshire coast they set up military posts and signal stations. One of these was at Filey, and others may have existed on those parts of the coast which have now gone. Outside the towns a number of Roman villas indicates how the Romans favoured the sheltered valleys of the edges of the Wolds.

In the sixth century the Saxons came. Entering by the Humber, Ouse and Derwent, they settled on the lower slopes of the Wolds and in the south and east parts of Holderness less marshy than the Hull valley. Place-names from this early settlement are the various '-inghams' along the north shore of the Humber and by the Roman road from Brough to York. The many '-ton' names represent continuing Saxon settlement in the sixth and seventh centuries, followed in the eighth-century by Scandinavian invaders. In the second half of the ninth century Danish settlers added their contribution in the many '-thorpe' names on the Wolds, representing a secondary settlement as the newcomers spread outwards from the existing farmsteads and hamlets.

Apart from the pattern of settlement and the names of the villages, very little historical fact comes down to us from those centuries. One event was the visit of Paulinus and his missionaries in A.D. 627, when they are supposed to have met King Edwin at Londesborough.

By the time of the Norman Conquest the present sites of almost all the villages and towns in the East Riding had been established. In 1066 was fought at Stamford Bridge a great battle between the English King Harold and the Norse leader, Harald Hardrada, which ended in an English victory, whose sweet taste was soured a few days later when the English army was defeated by William at Hastings.

The coming of the Normans made little difference to life in the villages of the East Riding, for farming had to continue no matter who was the overlord. Anglo-Saxon work survived in some of the churches – the west tower of Skipwith, at Wharram-le-Street, and St Mary Bishophill Junior in York. There are fragments of cross-heads, a nearly complete shaft at Nunburnholme, and the famous frid-stool in Beverley Minster.

Norman churches dominate the villages at North Newbald, Kirkburn, Goodmanham, and Garton-on-the-Wolds, but mostly the Norman work in the churches is in a doorway, a tower arch, or chancel arch. Nevertheless, the East Riding does contain some of the finest of our parish churches. Apart from York Minster, there is Beverley Minster and St Mary's, Beverley, Bridlington Priory, the steepled splendours of Hemingborough and Patrington, and the grandeurs of Hedon and Howden, all showing the glory of English Gothic. Many centuries later saw the Gothic Revival restorations by Street, Pearson and Temple Moore.

The East Riding boasts only one castle of importance, at Wressle, but motte-and-bailey earthworks provide evidence of a wide dispersal of Norman baronial power, those at Skipsea being the site of the castle of the Seignior of Holderness. At Paull Holme, near Hull, a late fifteenth-century tower-house of brick is a rare survivor from the days of threats from coastal raids.

Only slightly more numerous are the remains of the monastic houses, of which Kirkham Priory is by far the most significant, although not much survives above the ground compared with the more famous abbeys at Rievaulx and Fountains. But Kirkham's situation in the most delightful section of the valley of the Derwent adds to its undoubted appeal. The Derwent gorge is geologically important, having been carved by the melt-waters of Lake Pickering as an overflow channel draining that huge sheet of water southwards to the Ouse.

Part of the Augustinian Priory at Bridlington has been adapted for use as the parish church, while Watton was perhaps the most unusual, being a double house for canons and nuns. Part of the prior's guest-house forms the basis of the present country house. Small communities of nuns lived at Nunburnholme, Nunkeeling, Thicket, and Wilberfoss, with the Cistercian order at Swine, close to the only Cistercian abbey in the East Riding, at Meaux, in the valley of the Hull. It was monks from Meaux who were responsible for some of the early drainage systems of the low-lying lands around their abbey, and south-east towards the Humber.

Throughout Yorkshire the suppression of the monasteries was an unpopular act, for although they were not being very well managed, their abbots, priors, monks and nuns were generally friendly towards the rural population. Thus, when the rising known as 'The Pilgrimage of Grace' began in Lincolnshire in 1536, it soon spread to Yorkshire, where it received strong support.

Until about 1700 about half of the East Riding was a landscape of open fields, particularly on the Wolds, where you could have travelled for miles without seeing a settlement – or even a hedge. It was virtually one enormous sheep-walk. Gradually, first in the vales and Holderness and much later on the Wolds, enclosures began to be made and a field pattern established, a process which, between 1730 and 1810, added perhaps 6,000 miles of hedges to the East Riding landscape – mainly of hawthorn, although elder was used in very exposed places and willow in some low-lying areas.

During the eighteenth century many landowners enclosed and developed their estates, planted shelter-belts and woodlands, and added hedgerow trees. They laid out their new landscaped parks, rebuilt their houses, and were instrumental in providing some new roads. The Parliamentary enclosures brought about the rebuilding of many farms in the middle of their new fields, away from the villages. You see this characteristic today in the many examples of sturdy, brick-built Georgian farmhouses, sheltered by trees, standing well back from the roads of the Riding.

Many of the roads over the Wolds are very wide – 60 feet between the hedges, with only 12 feet of metalled surface – a characteristic of new roads created at the time of the enclosures. Bushes sometimes grew on the grass verges, and although travellers may have appreciated the great width of road it is doubtful if the local farmers and landowners did, for quite frequently the verges were used as campsites by gypsies or rubbish tips for villages – a misuse of verges not unknown today. However, they did provide grazing for the animals of commoners who had lost some of their rights with the enclosures. The roads linking the larger towns were largely the creations of the various Turnpike Trusts, some of whose original neat milestones still stand, usually as metal plates fixed to small stones.

Some of the old landscape survives. At Beverley Pastures and around Millington and Thixendale there is still pasture with gorse bushes as there has been for centuries. Patches of ridge and furrow can be seen near Sproatley and around the sites of some of the 120 or so deserted medieval villages of the East Riding, which make it one of the most rewarding areas of England for this particular landscape feature.

The East Riding is an agricultural county. Most of the Wold farms have 400–500 acres of land, half down to cereals, barley being popular followed by wheat; while root-crops, seed potatoes in particular – are on the increase. These give some help to the pheasants and partridges as well as contributing food supplies for the large sheep population. Suffolk cross ewes are favoured for breeding, large sheep being preferred as they are more hardy and able to withstand the bitterly cold winds which blow across the bare uplands during the winters. Since there are so many very small dales cutting into the Wolds, most farms have some land covering the steep sides of these narrow valleys which is rough grazing, the home of the hundreds of sheep and lambs which occupy them now as did their ancestors throughout the Wolds in past centuries.

The permanent flocks of today's Wolds comprise upwards of 200,000 ewes and lambs which are augmented by the very large numbers of store lambs bought in each autumn from the Border auction markets, or even from farther north. These are fattened-up during the months before Christmas to be replaced by others bought later, it being reckoned that one acre of land should be able to fatten 15–20 lambs. Some are still retained until early spring and sold as super-heavyweights, but there has been a declining demand for these. The store-lambs are taken off, the land is ploughed, and barley, usually, is sown.

Herds of dairy cattle are not so numerous on the Wold farms as in the Vale of York or on the Holderness clays. Just over half the East Riding's 140,000 cattle are on Wold farms, and although some may have 80–100 Friesians, it is more common to find much smaller herds than this. Mechanisation and a changing husbandry have brought about a big reduction in the former manpower staffing of Wold farms. Tractors and combines have increased. The cost of these items is such that they can be justified only when there is a big enough acreage of cereals – about 300 acres being regarded as a minimum. Drying units also add their stark lines to the smooth Wold contours – one of these being able to handle about 90 tons of corn a day, the product of just over 40 acres, the amount which can be cut in a day, all going well.

Inevitably, this increase in machinery on the cereal-growing parts of the Wolds has caused the grubbing-up of many hedges. So in places the landscape is reverting to its pre-enclosure picture of huge fields stretching to rolling horizons. Man's hand is always at work shaping the landscape, reminding us that a rural county such as the East Riding shows the work of fifty human generations over most of its face, and in some places, especially on the Wolds, the thin soil has been tilled and livestock pastured for over a hundred generations.

Against such a span, the growth of the towns is a very recent thing. Outside York, Beverley was for centuries the chief East Riding town, an important wool-marketing centre in the Middle Ages. Down Beverley Beck to the Humber and beyond to the continent sailed the merchants and the cargoes; to Beverley came Flemish immigrants bringing new blood, and new ideas which included the manufacture and use of bricks for building. Hull and the area around was the first part of Britain to use bricks in its major buildings. This was an important factor in the East Riding, for the county lacks any good building stones. Chalk has been used at Flamborough and at one or two Wold villages, while the belt of limestone and sandstone along the western foot of the Wolds is responsible for the visual appeal of villages such as Langton, Settrington, Bishop Wilton, and Howsham. In the southern part of the Derwent valley some half-timbered houses are a reminder that wood was much more plentiful two or three centuries ago. But throughout the Riding, brick predominates. Towns, villages, and scores of farmhouses, nearly all of eighteenth- and nineteenth-century date, show the good use of this most common building material. Since much of the modern in-filling, as well as the new housing estates of the dormitory villages of Humberside, are also of brick, there are few discordant notes.

The industrial revolution affected the East Riding less than many other areas; canals were cut towards Driffield and Pocklington, navigation was improved on the Derwent, and important drainage schemes improved the land of The Carrs in both the north and the south of the area. George Hudson, the 'Railway King', was an East Riding man, and was responsible for most of the railways built east of York in the 1840s. By the mid 1860s, the East Riding network was complete; a century later half its tracks had been taken up.

York. *Top: left* (1) the medieval city wall and view to Minster; *right* (2) the Central Hall, York University, built 1962–5; *Bottom* (3)   St William's College, originally a prebendal house, converted c. 1460 into a house of chantry priests.

Introduction

Although Hull had been growing as a trading port since before 1300, the advent of the railways saw its real rise to national importance as our major fishing port. Before that happened it had been the base of our Arctic whaling fleet, and now its interests have diversified, its prominence assured as the gateway to Europe, and the commercial and administrative capital of the huge new county of Humberside. The M.62 is reaching out towards Hull from the industrial West Riding, and in 1976 it will be linked directly to Lincolnshire and the south with the completion of the new Humber Bridge.

In a roll-call of famous people the East Riding has its share, especially in the arts. Alcuin, of York, was one of the greatest Saxon scholars; Andrew Marvell was born at Winestead in Holderness, while the two great contemporaries who influenced English architecture, William Kent and the Earl of Burlington, came from Bridlington and Londesborough respectively. An early conservationist in York was the painter William Etty, and nearer our own time W. H. Auden was a York man, while Rudston was the birthplace and home of Winifred Holtby. The pioneer woman aviator, Amy Johnson is commemorated in her birthplace, Hull; perhaps in due course a similar honour might be given to the actor Ian Carmichael, a Hull man. Perhaps best-known of all the East Riding's sons are the reformers – the Sykes of Sledmere in the field of agriculture, Wilberforce with his campaign to abolish slavery, and Seebohm Rowntree who fought to eliminate poverty in York and our other large cities.

I cannot claim allegiance to the East Riding, either by birth or adoption. But, having spent half my life just beyond the North Riding boundary, on the other side of the Tees, I have visited the various Ridings as frequently as possible. While admitting a strong preference for the Pennines and their lovely dales, and an equal fondness for the moors of the North Riding, I have come to a real affection for the softer lines of the East Riding, not least because it is so much a man-made landscape. And man has done a pretty good job with it.

I have assumed that most people will see the East Riding by car. Its roads are certainly better than its footpaths; although

4.   York Minster interior: the nave facing east, begun 1291. The 14th-century vault was replaced in 1840 after a fire.

there is an official long-distance track, 'The Wolds Way', this is not always definitive. Footpath signs are few and far between, but wherever it is possible to do so I advise some explorations on foot. The secrets of the Wolds and the splendours of the chalk cliffs offer their own rewards to the walker. York and Hull are best explored on foot, and both cities have plenty of good, cheap car-parking space.

York is the obvious gateway to the East Riding but it is not a good centre. Filey or Bridlington, although well to the north, can be useful for exploring the coast, while for the inland areas Great Driffield and Pocklington are probably best situated. But because Beverley was for centuries the capital of the Riding, and is such a lovely town in its own right I should make it the centre from which to see this unexpectedly rewarding 'thirding' of Yorkshire.

CHAPTER TWO

York
The City for all Seasons

'This is York. This is York.' The amplified nasal tones of the station announcer could not remove the thrill of that simple statement. I was fortunate to visit York for the first time one spring day about 30 years ago, when there was little traffic on the roads. I was fortunate, too, in arriving there by train, for when I emerged from the great station with its superbly curving lines of roof and platforms, I saw the walls of the city, silvery white on their grassy ramparts gay with the gold of daffodils. It was love at first sight, an affection that has deepened with the years. But now, when I go to York it is by road, and the entry to the city is a tedious, noisy, and irritating business which dulls the joy of anticipation. The railway travellers still have the best of it.

King George VI said 'The history of York is the history of England'. In 1971 York celebrated the 1900th anniversary of its founding. At the far end of that long tunnel of time a warlike tribe, the Brigantes, occupied most of the north of England, and by A.D. 71 the Romans had conquered the southern half of Britain. To subjugate the Brigantes, the Emperor Vespasian ordered his Roman governor, Quintus Petillius Cerialis, commanding the ninth legion, to move his army northwards from Lincoln. He did so and quickly established a base camp in the triangle of land formed by the meeting of the two rivers, Ouse and Foss, in A.D. 71. This temporary base became a permanent fortress, Eboracum, enclosed by earthen banks and timber walls.

The next governor, Agricola, completed Cerialis's work, and during Emperor Trojan's reign his fortress was rebuilt with stone walls, A.D. 108–9. The ninth legion was still at York, but by A.D. 122 it had been replaced by the sixth. Within the next five years Hadrian's Wall had been built. York became an important garrison town of the Roman Empire, and with Chester controlled the peace in the northern half of Britain until the end of the second century, when it was wrecked by rebelling tribesmen at a time when many Roman troops were out of the town. Eventually, order was restored and York rebuilt by the Emperor Severus, who died there in 211.

In 306 Emperor Constantine Chlorus died at York. His son Constantine being there, he was proclaimed Emperor of Western Rome, the only British proclamation of an emperor. Thus it was in York that Constantine the Great began the rule which would result in his becoming the first Christian emperor, the founder of Constantinople, and one of the most famous of all Romans. But by 406, the legions were withdrawn, and Roman rule in Britain had ended.

They left behind in York the shape of their fortress, a rectangular area with walls, four gates, and two straight streets intersecting at the military headquarters, the town's most important building. Via Principalis entered from the north by what is now Bootham Bar, and followed the line of the present Petergate to King's Square. Via Praetoria started where St Helen's Square now stands, and followed roughly the line of the present Stonegate. Stand now at the busy crossing of these two streets, and you are above the central crossroads of the Roman town. Just to the north-east was the Principia, the headquarters building, on the site now occupied by York Minster.

Roman York lay north of the River Ouse. Beyond Lendal Bridge, in a corner of the Museum Gardens is the Multangular Tower, the west angle tower of the Roman fortress wall, adjoining a 100-foot length of the wall. This reaches a height of 17 feet and includes a characteristic band of red tiles, but lacks its parapet. Its interior walls show the masonry in a better condition. By walking along the wall northwards past the King's Manor to Bootham Bar, continuing on the medieval wall to the corner of Lord Mayor's Walk, then to Monk Bar east of the Minster, you have followed two sides of the perimeter of the Roman fortress. Its other half has been obliterated by buildings, although fragments of Roman York survive. There is a magnificent collection of Roman finds in the Yorkshire Museum, and in the undercroft of the Minster.

Little is then known about York until the Saxons settled within its walls in the seventh century. In 627 King Edwin was baptised into the Christian faith by Paulinus, and built the first wooden church of York Minster on the site of the Roman Principia. Next century saw York as a European centre of learning with Alcuin its great teacher, but in 867 the town fell to Danish invaders. They created its use as a port, making it a trading centre, and built earth ramparts to the walls, as well as giving it some of today's street names, Goodramgate and Coney Street. In 944 Edmund recaptured York into Anglo-Saxon England.

During Norman times York became the second city in England. William the Conqueror visited it in order to subdue northern rebellions, and built two wooden castles on great earthen mottes, one each side of the Ouse. These mounds remain, as the site of Clifford's Tower, and the Baile Hill, covered by trees. York had been a bishopric since Saxon times, Paulinus being the first bishop, and a stone church had existed from about 670 until its destruction by fire at the Norman Conquest. Thomas of Bayeux, archbishop from 1070 to 1100 built the first Norman cathedral, replaced a century later by a larger one, but it was in medieval times that the present superb structure started to grow.

In the thirteenth century the present city walls were built, with their embattled gateways. Protection for the soul was ensured by the founding of a great abbey, a priory, nunneries and friaries, and the building of more than 40 churches, so York quickly became one of the great religious centres in medieval England. To dominate it, Archbishop Walter de Grey planned a huge Gothic cathedral, and building started in 1220 with the south transept, completed 20 years later. The next 20 years saw the north transept completed, both being in the linear beauty of Early English. Between 1297 and 1310 came the octagonal Chapter House with its corniced roof unsupported by any central pillar. By 1338 the nave was finished, in Decorated dignity, but it took about 90 years to complete the beautiful choir, in Perpendicular style, by 1450. The twin west towers reached their carved and pinnacled glories to the sky by 1472, followed by the enormous central tower in 1480, so that York's greatest architectural and spiritual glory took two and a half centuries to build.

Early in 1967 York Minster was beginning to sink on its foundations. Its central tower, weighing 25,000 tons was given 15 years more to live. The east wall of the chancel was nearly three feet out of plumb. Mr Bernard Fielden, Surveyor to the Fabric, carried out a two-year examination, and presented a 500-page report. Restoration was soon under way; a £2 million appeal quickly received enormous world-wide support. Thousands of tons of concrete were poured into the Minster especially into its foundations, where huge bolts of stainless steel formed the basis of the gigantic underpinning operation. New discoveries were made, such as that in 1968 when, during the restoration of Archbishop Walter de Grey's tomb, his coffin was opened to reveal, beside his bones, an ivory-topped crozier, a silver chalice, and a jewelled ring valued at £20,000. These, together with a host of other finds, are on permanent display in the unique museum now in the undercroft, where concrete and stainless steel stand adjacent to restored foundations of Roman walling of the original Principia. In 1972 the five-year restoration was completed sufficiently for a joyous celebration in Minster, city, shire and country.

While the great Minster survives, restored, St Mary's Abbey has decayed into gentle ghostliness, white-walled in the Museum grounds. Founded by Stephen of Lastingham in 1080 it became the most important Benedictine monastery in the north, but only a little survives: part of the wall of the north aisle, part of the west wall, and a pier arch of the crossing tower. Although the abbey lies outside the city walls, it has managed to retain more original monastic walling than any other English foundation. This, and its situation in the Museum garden, helps you to exchange the sounds of modern

York for the silences of an ancient sanctity. Lawns hide some of the abbey foundation, the footings of walls and piers reveal the outlines of monastic buildings, and down the bank towards the river the Hospitium, where the abbot entertained his guests, has been largely rebuilt and forms part of the museum.

Every third year St Mary's Abbey forms the setting for the revived York Mystery Plays. Dating from about 1340, there are 48 of these which were originally written and performed by the city's guilds; their themes span the Bible's story from Creation to the Last Judgement. Most of the 48 are still performed in modern adaptations, mainly by local citizens during a three-week period in mid-summer, the next performances being in 1976. Once more the centre window of the north wall becomes the Eye of Heaven, where God and His angels appear, first at the Creation, then at various times as Man moves through his story. Night falls over the city and the centuries; lighting effects add modern nuances to the old Mysteries, where medieval thought and humour leaven the deeper spiritual content.

Today we can look down on medieval and modern York from its walls. Their two and a half miles of limestone ramparts, on the green embankment, offer a two-hour circuit that spans six centuries. You can start anywhere, but since we have just been at St Mary's Abbey we may as well pick up the story at Lendal Tower, on the north bank of the Ouse, which formerly had a chain stretched across it here to prevent enemy vessels gaining access to the centre of the city. Beyond the Multangular Tower of the Roman wall is the little Anglian Tower, excavated in 1971, which is a survival from the seventh-century city.

Outside the wall near here is the King's manor, now part of the University, but originally the home of the Abbot of St Mary's, which, after the Dissolution, was used as the headquarters of the King's Council of the North. Part of the present structure dates from its rebuilding of 1540, but most of it was enlarged by the Earl of Strafford about 1630–40.

Bootham Bar is on the site of the old north-west gate into the city, and gives access to the footpath along the top of the wall. From here round to Monk Bar is the stretch which offers views to quiet gardens round the north side of the Minster. Mature chestnut trees add their gold of autumn to the silver massed masonry, and the white-walled houses of Minster Yard are foils to the gables of the Treasurer's House and Gray's Court. Outside the wall is the best remaining bit of the moat, now a grassy sward between wall and Lord Mayor's Walk with its lines of cars.

Monk Bar is the highest of the gateways, the carved stone men on its turrets poised to drop stones on to the busy street below, where pedestrians and traffic are frequently unaware of either the figures on top or the portcullis in its slot. Beyond Monk Bar is the remains of a Roman corner tower, and then Layerthorpe Bridge where there is a long gap to Red Tower. Here was marshy land in the old days, and the King's Fishpond, now drained and crossed by Foss Islands Road. The Red Tower is the only brick structure in the wall, and dates from 1490 although it is much restored.

Walmgate Bar is on the east of the city, directly opposite the main road to Hull and the coast. It is the only town gateway in York and in England to retain its barbican. On the inner, upper face of Walmgate is a wooden house added in Tudor times to give more living accommodation. A good stretch of the wall leads to Fishergate Bar which had been re-opened in 1827 to give access from the city to the Cattle Market then built outside the walls. At Fishergate Postern the wall temporarily ends, for the River Foss and the River Ouse, with the Castle Mound between them, provided their own defences. In the neck of land at the confluence a huge carpark fulfils its useful modern function of taking some of the visitors' traffic away from the streets within the walls, and encouraging an exploration of York on foot.

The thirteenth-century quatrefoil keep of Clifford's Tower looks down from its high, steep-sided motte on to Castle Yard, site of the former bailey and now occupied by the three great buildings facing inwards across the circular grassy lawn called 'The Eye of York'. Beyond the Ouse at Skeldergate Bridge, we pick up the medieval wall at Baile Hill. By Sadler Tower the wall turns a corner to run parallel to Nunnery Lane with another large carpark along the outer base of the tenth-century embankment. Micklegate Bar is the city's first gateway seen by visitors approaching from the west. Above the Norman archway were once displayed the severed heads of traitors; now the restored heraldic arms look colourfully down from the gleaming stone.

Beyond Micklegate Bar the wall turns another corner at Tofts Tower, and then enters one of its best stretches. In front the Minster draws the eye along the battlemented line of the wall. The defensive bulwark, sturdy yet sinuous, was a physical protection against the invader, the Minster a majestic Gothicism to the Glory of God. Here is the history of England.

Within the city wall is the great concrete block of Hudson House, a British Rail headquarters, on the site of the little Victorian station of 1841 and overlooking the burial-ground of the many victims of a cholera plague in 1832. Outside the wall is the curving 'modern' York station of 1877, its enormous size symbolic of the city's importance as the major railway centre outside London. York could have remained a quiet county town with its population under 20,000. But at the beginning of the railway age, a York draper, George Hudson, recognised the vital importance of its position. Midway between London and Edinburgh, between the port of Hull and the industrial West Riding and Lancashire, close to the South Yorkshire coalfield, and a gateway to the seaside resorts of the coast, York was the obvious centre for a network of railway lines. And such it became, after Hudson met George Stephenson. Between 1839 and 1849 the 'Railway King' built his empire, ranging from York to Berwick, to London, to Hull, to Skipton, with the many branches inter-connecting.

Here, the outer bank of the rampart shows its brilliant daffodil tapestry each spring, while on its inner face are some formal flowerbeds, which provide a colourful foreground to the most-photographed view in York. The stream of traffic surges into the city by Station Road, bridged by the line of the walls, which end a short way farther on at the Barker Tower, on the southern side of Lendal Bridge. The steps beside it led to the ferry which crossed the river at this point.

Throughout the circuit of the walls you are aware of the way in which the streets of medieval York (outside the Roman nucleus) follow no pattern. You are aware of the towers and spires of the many city churches breaking the skyline; you are also aware of how little the citizens of York seem to bother about this marvellous asset to their city. But more than anything else, you are aware of how the height of the wall above the city's streets is sufficient to reduce the noise of York. The sounds do not appear to travel upwards; the quietness on the walls adds to their feeling of timelessness.

The streets themselves take us, through their names – all on excellently lettered name-plates, incidentally – to the city's Scandinavian past. Goodramgate, coming in through Monk Bar, is 'Guthram's Street', and contains the oldest houses in York on its north side. Spurriergate, nearer the centre, is the spur-makers' street, while Whip-ma-Whap-ma Gate is York's shortest street and probably the site of the old pillory, or whipping post. Micklegate means 'great street', a name thoroughly justified by its importance, continuing the way into the city across the only bridge then in existence. Now, its graceful curving gradient contains some of the best Georgian town houses and as good a range of shops as any of York's streets, although there is some less happy in-filling.

Low and High Petergate lead directly to the great Minster of St Peter, the division between them being marked by Stonegate, the original crossroads of Roman York. Minerva, Goddess of Wisdom, with her owl and a pile of books, looks down on this historic corner of York, an appropriate reminder that this area of the city was the home of the bookbinders and booksellers, a continuing tradition today. This was the first of York's streets to be made free of traffic so that now it has come into its own, a delight for visitors, with a fine wealth and variety of shops, many of them occupying the old town houses of rich merchants, the fine half-timbered Mulberry Hall of 1434 being one of these. Stonegate is one of England's most historic and intimate streets.

The Shambles leads off King's Square at the lower end of Petergate. Almost over-restored, it still retains its medieval flavour, the wooden shelves in front of some of its shop-windows, and the hooks above them being reminders of the days when butchers displayed their meat here, shadowed by the overhanging storeys. Behind the Shambles is Newgate Market, where the traditional open-air-market sale of goods continues in its ancient pattern.

At the southern end of the Shambles is Pavement, the first paved street in York. Herbert House of 1557 shows some exquisite carving on its old timbers. Like so many of York's old buildings, it bears a neat, well-designed plaque with brief details of its history. From Pavement, Parliament Street runs northwards to St Helen's Square, the pivot of more modern York, with the red-painted elegance of the Mansion House surveying it from the west.

This official home of the Lord Mayor during his term of office dates from about 1725, and is attributed to the Earl of Burlington. Georgian pilasters and pediment have looked down on two and a half centuries of the city's life where now engines' throb has replaced the horses' clop, but inside the beautiful stateroom dinners are still held by candlelight. In the Mansion House, too, are kept the rich plate and regalia of the city, and these, like the interior of the house itself, can sometimes be seen by prior appointment.

By the fourteenth century York was the largest English city outside London, with over 10,000 inhabitants. A weavers' guild had been established as early as the twelfth century, and in the centuries that followed many more guilds of the various craftsmen were added, until they numbered about 60. These medieval guilds controlled much of the city's trade, ensured that the work of craftsmen was up to standard, and, like present-day Trade Unions, looked after the interests of their members. Although many guilds had their own halls, their common meeting-place was the Guildhall.

Behind the Mansion House the present Guildhall replaces the original fifteenth-century building which was largely destroyed during an air raid in 1942, only part of the stone walls surviving, and forming the shell of today's structure. Great oak pillars, each cut from a single tree, support the timbered roof where carved bosses, heraldic arms of royalty and city, add their touches of colour. The history of York is pictured in the panels of the great stained-glass window, and to its right, by the dais, a bronze plaque given by New York in 1924 expresses the friendship and goodwill of the old city's godchild in the New World.

Ceremonies and civic occasions through the centuries have graced the Guildhall. Royalty has been entertained, and now exhibitions, concerts and meetings are held regularly. It was appropriate that the York Civic Trust, which has done so much to make the face of York what it is today, should have held its Silver Jubilee dinner in the Guildhall in 1971, the first banquet in the new building.

An inner room escaped the 1942 destruction. Its panelled walls and richly decorated ceiling witnessed the counting of a £200,000 payment to the Scots by Cromwell for their help in the Civil War. Another room is the Victorian Council Chamber. Its view overlooking the Ouse helps to relieve the gloom of its sombre woodwork. The reorganisation of local government in 1974 demoted York, of all places, to a District Council. Only its 39 councillors and the Lord Mayor meet in the Council Chamber, for York is now merely part of the North Yorkshire County Council based on Northallerton, where the big decisions are made and from where the purse strings are controlled. Northallerton has the County Hall, but York had its Commonhall, predecessor of the Guildhall, and a passage beneath the Guildhall is called Commonhall Lane. A stone-flagged medieval alleyway leading down to the river, this was the old water-gate to the City, on the site of the Roman ford, and the way by which the magnesian limestone from Tadcaster quarries was brought into York, taken along Stonegate, and used in the building of the Minster.

The Merchant Adventurers' Hall in Piccadilly, is one of the surviving halls of a medieval guild, dating from the fourteenth century. Colourful banners of many guilds add their heraldic content to the splendid roof, the wooden floor is happily uneven, and old portraits stare from the walls. Beneath the Great Hall, about 90 feet long, is the undercroft, massively oak-pillared, and, until last century, cubicled for guild pensioners to live in.

Smaller, but equally impressive, standing almost in the shadow of the city wall in Aldwark, is the Merchant Taylors' Hall. Seventeenth-century brickwork hides its fourteenth-century timbering and the building was completely restored recently, ensuring that the hall lives as a building regularly in use for various social functions. The Merchant Taylors' Company was incorporated in 1661 when three craft guilds were amalgamated – Taylors, Drapers and Hosiers.

Aldwark is one of the most run-down parts of York, and the Esher proposals for conservation in the city have outlined the particular problems here as not so much a question of filling in gaps, but of identifying the few worthwhile fragments which survive, and building harmoniously round them. Since 1954, restoration work has been carried out in York, but the essential stimulus to it resulted from the Historic Buildings Act of 1962, allowing local authorities to make grants. The passing of the 1967 Civic Amenities Act brought about the Town Scheme idea creating the whole historic centre of the city a Conservation Area in which many properties have benefited from grants.

Fewer than half of York's medieval churches have survived the toll of the centuries' decay. Of those remaining, some are no longer places of worship, some have become derelict, and for others a secular use has been found to give them a new lease of life. Many of the 19 medieval churches within the walls are kept locked except for services. All Saints, Pavement, is characterised by its openwork tower of the late fifteenth century, serving as a beacon to travellers outside York. Holy Trinity in Micklegate was once part of a Benedictine Priory, and has stocks in the churchyard. St Helen's in Stonegate was the church of the medieval glass craftsmen, and is now used as the city's civic church; Holy Trinity in Goodramgate, behind York's oldest row of houses, retains its box-pews, a rare saddleback roof and some finely lettered tombstones. In Coney Street, marked by the wonderful projecting clock crowned by a sailor known as the 'Little Admiral', St Martin-le-Grand was gutted during an air raid. Partly rebuilt, it now shows a happy union of fifteenth- and twentieth-century architecture, and the adjoining paved garden is a shrine of remembrance. St Michael's in Spurriergate still tolls its curfew bell each evening at 8 p.m., while in the churchyard of St George's, George Street, is a modern replacement headstone to Richard (Dick) Turpin.

One of York's most famous sights is the Castle Museum, occupying part of the site of the former Castle, opposite Clifford's Tower. On the east side is the Women's Prison, designed by John Carr in 1780 to balance his beautiful Assize Courts opposite, of 1777. Facing north is the older Debtors' Prison of 1705, probably by one of Vanbrugh's pupils. The two prisons now house the Castle Museum, one of the great folk museums of the world, gradually developed here since 1935, when a country practitioner from Pickering gave his unique collection to the City of York. From early this century Dr J. L. Kirk had collected bygones of all sorts, everyday objects used by the country people he met. Begging many, buying some, taking others instead of his fees, he slowly built up the finest collection in England. When he handed it over to York it took three years to prepare the Women's Prison, transport Dr Kirk's collection and house it in its new surroundings. Inside, a Victorian street has been rebuilt in the old exercise yard, complete with shops, a coaching-house, and a hansom cab. This is merely one of a host of delights in which you not only look through the homely windows of history, but for a little while live in it. York's Castle Museum is a magical, marvellous Time Machine that works, and its founder is remembered in the name of one of its streets, Kirkgate.

There is more to the city of course, than the medieval core. Two household names in the world of chocolate and sweets started in York as small family businesses in the eighteenth century. In 1725 a Mary Tuke opened a grocer's shop, which later turned to the manufacture of cocoa and chocolate, the business being transferred in 1862 to Henry Rowntree. 1767 saw the start in St Helen's Square of a confectionary business, which later became J. Terry and Sons, whose 'front' shop is still in the Square, the factory now operating from large neo-

Georgian buildings out on the Bishopthorpe Road. Rowntree's factory is on the northern outskirts of the city in a complex of buildings specially designed at the end of the last century.

A mile further out from the Rowntree factory is New Earswick, which started as a community early this century, largely as a result of Seebohm Rowntree's social survey into poverty in central York in 1900. The Joseph Rowntree Village Trust guided New Earswick into life as a small garden city where people in all types of work could live in healthy conditions, but without a public house.

Space does not allow me to give a roll-call of York's famous men and women, or of all its buildings. I can only touch on some aspects of the city and suggest you discover the extra details from some of the excellent guides and books that are available. But if your time allows it, explore beyond the walls, northwards along the Georgian elegance of Bootham, southwestwards by the Tadcaster Road to Knavesmire, that great common pasture, part of which now houses the 'Ascot of the North' where part of Carr's original grandstand of 1754 has been re-erected in the present paddock.

We have been immersed in the pageant of history so long in York that it is time we left the city to its memories and hopes. Much of its future will be bound up with the University founded in 1963, at Heslington. Since this is on our way into the East Riding we can pause for a quick walk round the campus, knowing we shall be welcome provided we do not go into the University buildings. The campus covers a 190-acre site, the various buildings being grouped round a central lake. Imaginative planning, thoughtful landscaping, and good design all combine to produce what is probably the most visually satisfying of all the new universities. One public road crosses the site in a shallow cutting, and throughout the campus, pedestrians and cars are well separated. Collegiate, so that every member of the University, staff or student, is a member of one of the six colleges, Alcuin, Derwent, Goodricke, Langwith, Vanbrugh, and Wentworth, each in its own building. Among the rest of the buildings, the Central Hall stands out, a half-octagon by the lake, its upper storeys cantilevered above the water, and surmounted by an aluminium roof – exciting modern architecture in a beautiful setting. The administrative headquarters of the University is at Heslington Hall, a Victorian rebuilding of a Tudor House. We turn left at the crossroads, to find ourselves on the A.1079 and soon take the A.166 across the Wolds to Great Driffield and the coast for a sniff of the sea. York may be the gateway to the East Riding, but its longest boundary is the coast, from Filey to the Humber. From there, like the early settlers, we shall explore gradually inland.

5. Filey Brigg: looking inland from the wave-lashed limestone shelf which juts a mile out into the North Sea.

CHAPTER THREE

Filey to Bridlington
The Coast of Chalk

The North Riding coast south of Scarborough is not of 'Enterprise Neptune' quality. Scarring rashes of caravan settlements and other holiday building contrast with some delightful small bays, but once the East Riding boundary is passed, a mile north of Filey, Nature dominates, and even the main road from Scarborough, the A.165, keeps a mile from the cliffs, which here are nearly 200 feet high. One of the Countryside Commission's long-distance footpaths, the Cleveland Way, technically ends at the Riding boundary, but there is a right of way from there to Filey Brigg, and this is the best and most exhilarating approach to the East Riding coast.

As you approach Filey from the north there are magnificent views across the crescent of Filey Bay, with the chalk cliffs of Speeton and Bempton six miles away and Flamborough lighthouse a sharp accent against the distant skyline. Filey itself sits neatly in the northern part of the arc, presenting the best grouping of sea-front buildings on the Yorkshire coast. But before looking more closely at the town, you must explore the Brigg. If you have walked southwards along the cliffs you have had the Brigg in front of you, nosing its low rocky ledges into the North Sea. If, however, you have arrived at Filey by road I suggest you seek the Country Park which has so sensibly been established on the cliffs above Filey Brigg.

Filey Brigg is by far the most exciting and dramatic feature on this stretch of coastline; a natural breakwater, where generations of locals and increasingly of visitors, have walked along

Bridlington. *Top left* (6) the west front of Priory Church; *right* (7) Bayle Gate: the west face, 1388, of the only surviving monastic building. *Bottom* (8) 18th-century shop fronts in the High Street.

its limestone ledges, and have been salt-sprayed by the crashing breakers. The obvious way out on to the Brigg is from the cliffs of red boulder-clay, ridged and contorted. On these cliffs the new Country Park provides plenty of space, amenities, and a Caravan Park for touring vans well back from the 'day visitor' area nearer the edge.

There is an easy track down to the Brigg with steps cut in the steeper places. Ideally, you should explore the Brigg when the tide is nearly out, and a mile of the Lower Calcareous Grit reaches out to sea. There are rock-pools galore – one of them, beneath the cliffs to the north, is called the Emperor's Bath, a beautiful pool of clear blue water, filled by each fresh tide, and with a natural rocky amphitheatre above. Filey Brigg shows its sterner aspect when the wind is in the north or north-west, and the wind-whipped waves surge and crash over the rocky platforms. In a really rough sea, of course, Filey Brigg is savage and dangerous, and has claimed many victims. At its seaward end many a coble of sailing days has been battered and overturned by the strength of the tides' torrents over submerged rocks. Yet on such days of northerlies you can sit in the lee of the cliffs, basking in warm sunshine, and watch the gentle white arcs of the breakers curving in across the sheltered sands. Fortunate is such a town with so splendid a natural breakwater as the Brigg, and in the 1850's Filey really set out to develop itself as a seaside resort.

The old part of Filey lies near St Oswald's Church, which stands on the northern brow of Church Ravine, a wooded glen, originally the boundary between the North and East Ridings, that leads down the northern edge of the town to the Coble Landings. From Church Street an iron bridge crosses the ravine to an extensive churchyard and the finest church in this part of the Riding. It belonged to Bridlington Priory, and dates mainly from late Norman to thirteenth-century times, with the addition of fifteenth-century battlements. The tower is as sturdy as a castle keep, and crowned by a gilded fish weathervane. Inside, the northern saints, Oswald, Aidan and Cuthbert are portrayed on the reredos, together with Paulinus and a slave boy at his feet. One window – the Fishermen's Window –

shows Christ calling Simon Peter and Andrew, and was given by the townsfolk of Filey to commemorate those many men from the town who have gone down to the sea in ships, and have not returned.

Church Street should be the best street in Filey, narrow, with cobbles down one side bordering a descending row of houses. These are mainly three-storey, two-bay buildings of Georgian brick, the lower ones being smaller, with roof-lines pleasantly mixed and façade details good, so one wonders by what touch of genius a very ugly, swan-necked, concrete lamp-standard was sited in the position where it is most visually damaging. Surely, one or two discreet wall-mounted lights would have been the obvious solution.

Queen Street runs eastwards from Church Street, and near the corner a pair of seventeenth-century cottages house the Folk Museum. The Filey Urban District Council restored them in 1970, and the Filey Lions decorated them for the Filey Local History Society who runs the Museum. Above one of the doorways is an inscribed stone dated 1696, bearing a coat-of-arms and the admonition 'The Fear of God be with You'. Inside there are models of lifeboats and lifeboatmen's gear, old costumes, implements and utensils, pieces of pottery, bottles, beach pebbles, weaving implements and pictures of sea rescues.

Filey presents a gracious front to the sea. The cliffs are not high, but the buildings along the shallow curve of The Crescent compensate for this. Six white stuccoed blocks date from Filey's birth as a seaside resort, 1840–1850. Greek Doric porches grace the earliest block which has a Regency iron balcony along its entire length. Beyond The Crescent are more good seaside villas so that there is an almost continuous front of good buildings which are hotels or guest-houses. No shops break the sequence, and therefore there are no advertisements, street posters or pictures, for the commercial part of Filey lies behind the sea-front façade, a gridiron pattern of streets busy with shops and people. On the front, well-kept gardens, trimmed and gay with formal flowers, separate the buildings along The Crescent from the edge of the low cliffs. Here walk the older visitors to the town, here dogs are exercised, a putting-green is patronised, and the men look out to sea.

Charlotte Brontë used to lodge at Cliff House, from where she wrote many letters to her home at Haworth, and to her friends. Canon Cooper, the walking parson, who was a much-loved Vicar of Filey for over 50 years commented once that during the height of the holiday season you could see at a glance at least a quorum of the House of Lords! Prince Louis of Battenburg and Princess Alice, granddaughter of Queen Victoria, were at Filey in 1900.

Although holiday-makers' habits have changed, Filey has adapted to them. Last century it was usual for a fairly rich family to take over a large house, bringing their own Nanny and servants with them. A later generation favoured the boarding-house, the guest-house, charges graded according to position relative to the sea-front. Now the demand is for holiday flatlets where families cook their own meals, while the more modern alternative is chalets, again rented on a self-catering basis. As a result of the increased mobility of more people, and the constant popularity of Filey among folk from the industrial West Riding, weekenders are on the increase, and the holiday season lasts longer.

We started this little tour of Filey by the Brigg and there we shall finish it, by walking to the north end of The Crescent, turning inland along Belle Vue Street, along Hope Street, and then down the steep hill of Cargate, taking us to the Beach. North along here, and at the bottom of Ravine Road, are the Coble Landings. Hauled up on a large concrete ramp are the Filey fishing cobles, bright with paint, high-prowed, square-sterned, lovely of line, and sure of purpose. In the early mornings of summer, big tractors drag them down the beach, they are heaved out into the breakers and head off for the fishing grounds, drifting for salmon, potting for crab and lobster, and returning after daylight, to be tractor-hauled, stern-first, up to their roosts. When they go off to winter fishing they long-line for haddock and cod. Nearby, where a tiny Wyke called Wool Dale meets the shore, is the headquarters of the Filey Sailing Club.

The main road south from Filey, the A.165, leads quite directly to Bridlington, about ten miles away, gradually leaving the coast. Billy Butlin established one of his earlier holiday camps on the low-lying ground of Hunmanby Moor, three miles south of Filey, but Hunmanby village is some distance away to the west of the main road.

Once a market town, this is now a large, friendly, welcoming place. The large open space of Cross Hill near the top of the village retains its old market cross close to a colourful War Memorial Garden in front of the Hall. But its former importance has long since gone. A coaching inn and some attractive eighteenth-century houses, white-painted, dormered, and pantiled, constitute a good grouping along the south and west sides of Cross Hills. Two of the houses have stones above their doorways carved in the form of stags' heads coming out of a crown, the device of the Osbaldestons, who lived at Hunmanby Hall for 200 years. Their former home is now part of a girls' school, standing back from the road, its late seventeenth-century brickwork still prominent among the trees. The main entrance to the Park is lower down the street, an impressive archway of stones hewn from the rocks of Filey Brigg early last century, but looking much more ancient.

At the entrance to the churchyard, at the 'top of the town' is the Bayley Garden. During my visit it was riotous with summer roses; a little shelter fronted a neat lawn, and a notice invited the public to sit and take their ease in this quiet spot near the heart of the village. On that summer morning of sunshine it was empty, as was the cool, dark interior of the church just behind. This has a cobbled floor to the south porch, a Maltese cross in the tympanum, a Norman tower and low chancel, and an enormous monument by the Fishers to William Osbaldeston, 1770. Hidden by trees nearby is the Vicarage, originally 1675, but added to by Archdeacon Francis Wrangham in 1803. This was necessary to house his library, for he journeyed the length and breadth of England collecting books, apparently irrespective of their cost. Until he built the new wing, they were piled everywhere, and he was mildly caricatured for it by Mrs Mitford, who knew him well. Sydney Smith used to visit

Wrangham, wrangle with him, and borrow his books. When the archdeacon died in 1842, the auction sale of his library lasted three weeks.

Stonegate leads down from above the church to Pinfold Green, where, earlier this century, pebbles which had been carted from the beach a couple of miles away were hammered by the local stone-breakers into a road-making material. Pinfold Green gained its name from the historic pinfold which still stands there, a circular structure of stone, originally used for impounding stray cattle, whose owners, when claiming them, had to pay a fine to the parish. Nearby, the brick lock-up dates from 1834, and is unusual in having two cells, each with its own door, for men and women delinquents. Its chief use was at the time of the Martinmas hirings.

Back on the main Bridlington road, Reighton is the next village, with a good view from the churchyard north across Filey Bay to the distant Brigg. The eighteenth-century house on the hill is Reighton Hall, where Hugh Edwin Strickland was born in 1811. Grandson of Edmund Cartwright, inventor of the power loom, young Strickland was a keen amateur geologist from an early age, when he spent many hours exploring the rocks and fossils of Speeton Cliffs just along the coast. Later in life he travelled on natural history expeditions in Africa and Asia, writing about his discoveries there. Unfortunately he was killed by a train while studying the rocks of a railway cutting near Gainsborough.

Speeton lies just off the main road, a mile past Reighton. It is a tiny village with one of the smallest churches in Yorkshire, which stands in a field, aloof at the eastern end of the village, near a farm and beyond a large pond, densely duck-weeded in high summer. The absence of a churchyard emphasises the smallness of the pagoda-like tower, only six feet wide at its base. Inside, the church is cleanly whitewashed – which almost hides the Norman chancel arch. In the east wall of the Sanctuary there is an old alms-box in the form of a small stone trough, with the remnants of its original fastening, but now without a lid.

The lane which leads to the church continues to the edge of

the cliffs, where it becomes an exciting path 400 feet above the sea. Here end the chalklands of Britain. Speeton Cliffs, Buckton Cliffs and Bempton Cliffs make a continuous majestic wall of white rock for six miles south-east to Flamborough Head. Walking the cliff-path is by far the best way to appreciate its magnificence, but if the famous Bempton Cliffs are the goal, then there is an easy way to approach them more closely by road. The B.1229 which left the main Bridlington road at Reighton, leads past Speeton to Bempton village, and continues to Flamborough. In the middle of Bempton a minor lane leads off to the north to Bempton Cliffs. It ends at a gate beyond which vehicles are not allowed. An adjacent field provides a limited area of free parking, and the cliffs themselves are less than a quarter of a mile away, along a chalky track.

Bempton Cliffs are in an area declared a Site of Special Scientific Interest, now partly in the ownership of the Royal Society for the Protection of Birds, partly in private ownership. They are a nature reserve because of the immense numbers of seabirds which breed on the cliffs. The R.S.P.B. have provided a neatly-designed wooden shelter near the carpark, with useful and informative posters designed to help visitors identify the birds and understand how they have colonised the cliffs in zones.

At the cliffs the R.S.P.B. has erected small enclaves of post-and-rail fencing on the projecting spurs, making safe observation areas giving superb views along the cliffs. The air is white with whirling wings, raucous with seabirds' calls and pungent with guano. Bempton Cliffs are not only the most southerly major seabird colony on the east coast, but the only mainland cliff in Britain where gannets breed. There is no finer sight than that of the arrogantly powerful grace of these soaring, swooping birds. The herring gulls are far more haphazard, much more noisy; kittiwakes, too, follow irregular flight-paths, while guillemots hurry around with their shorter, quicker wing-beats. Razorbills and puffins perch precariously by their tiny crevices and holes at various levels; gannets and fulmars occupy the upper ledges, and shags stand, dark singletons, near the foot of the cliffs.

You can walk the cliff path northwards to Speeton, or southwards to Flamborough with the sea and the birds for company, but only at Bempton are there such concentrated colonies. Although a Seabird Preservation Act of 1869 gave some relief to the birds at Bempton and Flamborough, the eggs were collected professionally for about 250 years prior to 1954, when the Wild Birds' Protection Act came into operation. Until then, the Bempton climbers were famous, swinging down the cliffs for hundreds of feet on the end of ropes fixed to metal posts firmly embedded in the ground. Although some eggs were eaten or sold to collectors, most were sent to Leeds where they were used in the manufacture of patent leather. As many as 130,000 guillemot eggs were collected in one year alone towards the end of last century. Now there is no climbing, no collecting, and the Bempton birds are free in their elements, the sky and the sea, and on the sentinel cliffs of chalk.

Bempton village is a rather crowded cluster of cottages in narrow, winding streets, with a large green slightly to the south. The tower of the church is crowned by an eight-sided lantern, while inside there is a rather rare survival in Yorkshire, a chancel screen which could be as late as 1829. Half a mile from the village is a railway station of 1846, and beyond, the tower of a mill breaks the skyline. Eastwards from Bempton, the B.1229 continues, as Flamborough Road to Flamborough itself.

The village is the capital of a few square miles of countryside known as Little Denmark because of its association with the Scandinavians who colonised it about A.D. 800. Little Denmark is separated from England by an immense linear earthwork, Danes Dyke, stretching for two and a half miles from Bempton Cliffs in the north to Sewerby Rocks in the south. This grass- and tree-covered entrenchment is, in some places, as much as 60 feet wide and 20 feet deep and was probably constructed for defensive purposes by the Brigantes, the Celtic tribe who peopled Yorkshire over 2,000 years ago.

Two roads enter Little Denmark – the B.1229 from Filey, and the B.1255 from Bridlington, converging at Flamborough, the centre of a fishing and farming community, whose population of 1,400 represents about three quarters that of the whole head-land. Although there is a lot of new building, some older houses of chalk, brick, or stone survive to retain a little of the former character of the village. But as is so often seen along this Yorkshire coast, the original is being engulfed by the encroach-ing tide of development, caravan sites near North Landing and Thornwick Bay making very unsightly scars, while poor-quality housing of between wars mars the approach to Flam-borough lighthouse. However, further indiscriminate development was prevented by Bridlington Corporation, who bought the headland in 1939.

St Oswald's Church retains its Norman chancel arch but most of the building is a restoration of 1864–69. The best feature is the rood-screen, which although much of it is renewed can still claim to be the most complete one in the East Riding. Indeed, only that at Hubberholme in Upper Wharfedale can better it. These two fifteenth-century rood-lofts are the only surviving medieval ones in Yorkshire, and probably owe their escape from the destroyers to the remoteness of their situation, virtually at the eastern and western extremities of the county.

In the church vestry is a pair of white paper gloves, formerly carried by the chief mourner at the funeral of a virgin of the parish, and subsequently hung on the rood-screen. The cus-tom ceased many years ago, these gloves being the last ones used. On a revolving stand in the north aisle is Flamborough's Book of Service which decoratively records the names of Flam-borians, who in any form gave service during the years 1939–45.

In a field to the north of the churchyard is the so-called 'Danish Tower'. Again, this is a misnomer, for the fragment is probably part of the keep of the fortified manor-house of the Constable family. In 1284 a de Lacy, Constable of Chester, took the name of his office as Lord of Flamborough, the family hav-ing been connected with the place since then. The grass-fringed and roofless walls are about 20 feet high, and there are traces of a vaulted undercroft. Licence to crenellate had been given in 1326 to Sir Marmaduke Constable. A later Sir Mar-maduke is commemorated by an old brass in the church, with

26 lines of inscription picked out in black letters. It was this Marmaduke who, at the age of 70, commanded the left wing of the English army at Flodden Field, where, it is said, he died from swallowing a frog while drinking water.

One of the vicars of Flamborough was the father of Andrew Marvell, the seventeenth-century poet, but another literary association with the village is less well known. In addition to *Lorna Doone*, R. D. Blackmore wrote more than a dozen other stories. One of these, *Mary Anerley*, published in 1880, is a tale of smuggling on the Yorkshire coast around the beginning of last century, and Flamborough Head features prominently in it.

The headland is two miles eastward from the village. The white finger of the lighthouse beckons at the far end of the B.1259, as it has done since 1806 when a Bridlington man, John Matson, using no scaffolding, built it in nine months. Called the 'new' lighthouse to distinguish it from its surviving predecessor, it is 92 feet high, stands 214 feet above the sea, some way back from the cliff edge, and its light is visible at a range of 21 miles. Prisms weighing three tons each float in a mercury bath and, rotating at a touch, magnify the 500 watt bulb to three quarters of a million candle power.

Not far from the road, the old beacon tower is a prominent landmark, and gives its name to one of the holes of the Flamborough Golf Course, the eleventh being known as the Tower hole. Built of the local chalk, it is octagonal in section, and was completed in 1674 as a coal-fire beacon tower.

Flamborough Head is more than merely the most famous promontory on the east coast. It is the last great outburst of the English chalklands, where the northern arc of the Wolds swings round and juts out five miles to meet the North Sea. The Yorkshire chalk is harder than that of southern England, and contains no flint, so that it is more resistant, and, as a wave-borne cutting agent, much less effective. Nevertheless, Flamborough Head is riddled with caves which no doubt made it a smugglers' paradise, especially since many of the caves are quite big enough to take a fishing coble. Almost every cave and promontory on the headland has been named. To quote *Mary*

Anerley:

'Half a league to the north of bold Flamborough Head, the billows have carved for themselves a little cove among the cliffs that are rugged, but not very high . . . but the hardy fishermen make the most of its scant convenience, and gratefully call it "North Landing".'

You can reach it today, by the B.1255 from Flamborough village, or more rewardingly by walking the cliff path from near the lighthouse, which ends in the usual clutter of bungalows, cafés and caravans. A steep track, which is definitely not for vehicles, continues down to the Landing itself, where the cobles are drawn up high on the chalky shingle, and the Flamborough lifeboat *Friendly Forester* is stationed.

Fishing is increasingly active at Flamborough, both the number of cobles in use and the value of their catches having steadily grown over the last ten years. Cod is predominant, with haddock, skate and ling quite common. The principal season starts about mid-October; fishing is by long-line from cobles, there being no drifters or trawlers. Fishermen often sell their catches on the beach to dealers who then arrange for the fish to be packed and sent to the station four miles away. Crab-fishing by pots extends from April to late summer.

Northwards along the coast, towards Thornwick Bay, are Church Cave and Smugglers' Caves, their interiors like dazzling white marble, colour-veined and cold. Southwards are even more caves, most of them accessible only by boat, although the largest and most famous, Robin Lythe's Cave, can be reached by a shore approach at low water. At its highest point, the central part of the roof of this cave is almost 50 feet above the ground.

The Flamborough cliffs look their most impressive from sea level. For the headland visitor, however, they offer their own reward, especially on the walk from North Landing to the headland. For a mile and a half the cliff path follows the indented coastline, where in small bays and inlets the clear water takes on a succession of semi-enclosed shapes, green-blue under a summer sky, with textured cliffs throwing light back into shadowed crevices.

In 1779 there was a sea battle off Flamborough Head between British and American forces, and this event is commemorated by a bronze plaque and toposcope near the lighthouse. In September of that year, John Paul Jones, commanding the American ship *Le Bonhomme Richard*, sailed down the east coast of Scotland in search of prey, flying the first 'Stars and Stripes' to be seen in Europe. Approaching the Yorkshire coast he learned that a fleet of Baltic merchant ships, escorted by two British men-of-war, was in Bridlington Bay. Jones knew he outgunned the British by almost two to one, so decided to attack them when they finally left the harbour. In full moonlight, on a calm sea, a murderous duel was fought with a great deal of bloodshed. Musket-fire, cannon-roar, and the screams of the wounded, reached the people of Flamborough, grandstanding the battle from the cliffs. Richard Pearson, the British commander, struck his colours but John Paul Jones' apparent triumph was short-lived, for his own ship went down soon afterwards, although he himself survived to pass most of the remainder of his life in relative obscurity.

The inscription on the plaque records that it was

. . . erected to serve as a reminder of the famous sea-battle which took place off the headland between American colonist John Paul Jones and Captain Sir Richard Pearson, R.N., John Paul Jones is regarded as the father of the U.S. Navy.'

The toposcope also reveals that the Greenwich Meridian passes about three miles east of the headland, and that both Land's End and John o'Groats are 362 miles away.

On the opposite side of Flamborough Head is South Landing, obviously favoured as a tiny harbour sheltered from the north-easterlies. Its situation is less striking, for the cliffs here are lower than those which embrace the North Landing. Nevertheless, a clifftop path enables an almost complete circuit of the headland to be enjoyed, with Flamborough village as starting and finishing point.

It is quite possible for motorists journeying down the coast from Flamborough to Spurn to miss Bridlington completely. The development of housing estates, and some light industries on the western edge of the town has allowed new roads to be built which serve as a very useful ring road round the north and west of the town. However, most folk would not want to miss Bridlington, which is not one place but really two – Old Town, grouped round the Priory Church, the Market Place and High Street, and Bridlington Quay a mile away, with its associated development as a busy, bustling, breezy seaside resort. Since Bridlington's story begins with the Priory Church, it is in that part that we shall start our exploration.

There was a church at Bridlington in Saxon times, but it was in 1114 that Walter de Gant founded a Priory for Austinian Canons there. Of his original monastery nothing remains *in situ* above ground, although in the north aisle of the church parts of the twelfth-century cloister have been re-erected. The usual approach to the Priory Church is by the Bayle Gate and the lawns of Church Green. The two west towers are quite different. Most of the older north-west tower is thirteenth-century, its neighbour is fifteenth-century in its lower stages, restored and greatly added to in 1876 by Sir Giles Gilbert Scott, who also added the top stage to the north-west tower. Between is the great west window, 55 feet high and about half that in width, presenting a slightly odd appearance because the part above the transom is set farther back in its frame.

The original church was over 330 feet long, but at the Dissolution its eastern half was pulled down, together with most of the monastic buildings. The nave had always been used by the people of Bridlington, so it was spared destruction to become the parish church. Lacking both choir and transepts its south wall has blind arcading where it once adjoined the Prior's Lodging. Although incomplete as a church, it possesses a cool, aloof dignity, flowing lines of stone leading the eye to a dark hammerbeam roof with king posts. Much of the woodwork on the floor of the church is modern, adze-finished oak from Robert Thompson's workshop at Kilburn.

The Priory became one of the wealthiest in the north of England. William of Newburgh was born at Bridlington and knew the Priory, although he spent most of his life at Newburgh, where he wrote his *History of English Affairs*. John of Bridlington, who was Prior in the fourteenth century, gained great renown as a holy and devout man, and was canonised by the Pope in 1401, with the result that kings, bishops and knights subsequently made pilgrimage to his shrine. Bridlington's last Prior was William Wood, who took part in the ill-fated Pilgrimage of Grace, for which he was hanged at Tyburn. The Priory was dissolved the following year, and most of the buildings savagely demolished. Only part of the church was spared together with the Priory Gatehouse, now called the Bayle Gate, of which much of the original has survived intact. Its lower storey is stone, the upper one brick, and it has two entrances on its west face, one for carriages, one for pedestrians, becoming one wide arch inside. The upper room is 60 feet long, with fine oak beams, and some modern tables by Thompson. It was used as a Court Room by the Priors, a prison during Cromwell's time, a nonconformist meeting-house during the Restoration, a soldiers' lodging during the Napoleonic Wars, and a school-room last century. Now it houses a small museum.

From the crossroads to the west of the Bayle Gate, High Street continues a westwards curve to the Market Place. This is the best street in Bridlington, with houses and shops nicely mixed. Some of the shops retain their Georgian window-fronts, many of them are antique shops, very few are modernly disfigured. The elegance is homely, sometimes almost decayed, but High Street still shows a rare unity although it would be better with a face-lift.

At right angles to High Street, the Market Place is a broad attractive street, wide as befits the old trading centre of the town. On its east side is New House, built in 1970 on the site of the old Corn Exchange which had for years been the centre of a prosperous agricultural community, the restoration being done by the Lords Feoffees of the Manor of Bridlington.

When the Manor of Bridlington passed from the canons to the crown, successive sovereigns were not really very grateful, for Bridlington meant a continuing battle with the sea. Consequently, some monarchs handed over the manor to their friends, though not all of them were keen to accept the gift. Eventually, a Mr William Corbett and twelve local men bought the manorial rights early in the seventeenth century for £3,260, and Charles I, thankful to have Bridlington off his hands, granted a charter allowing a private company to govern its affairs. Called the Lords Feoffees, they gained control of all public matters, and the rights to fairs and markets, a power which lasted until 1863 when it started to diminish in favour of the growing authority of local councils. The Lords Feoffees still meet twice a year, mainly to administer the various manorial properties of which they are the trustees. Bridlington natives, they are elected to their office which they then hold for life, even if they no longer live in the town.

Bridlington became a borough in 1899, with a mayor and corporation to govern its affairs. In 1934 they bought Sewerby Hall, about two miles to the north of the town, a handsome early Georgian house with porch and wings added about 1808. This public-spirited act of conservation of 40 years ago has paid good dividends, for the house and all its best features have been preserved, with a particularly fine staircase and many rooms retaining their 1714 decoration. It is open to the public; parts have been adapted for use as an art gallery and restaurant, and, in a room at the top of the staircase there is an impressive display of mementoes of Amy Johnson, Britain's pioneer woman of the air. Fifty acres of grounds surround Sewerby Hall including the original walled gardens, together with natural woodland and lawns.

Southwards from Sewerby is the shallow curve of North Sands, culminating at North Pier, the harbour separating the North Sands from those on the south. In its present form, Bridlington Harbour is largely as it was after it had been enlarged around 1850, and the Gypsey Race feeds into its landward end. There used to be a steady trade in the export of farm produce, livestock and coal, but today's small cargo vessels are more concerned with carrying fertiliser to the Channel Islands. Twelve of the oldest cobles on the east coast form part of the keel boat fleet, each one now, of course, run by a diesel engine. Their purpose is almost exclusively to take parties on hand-line fishing trips in Bridlington Bay. Sheltered by Flamborough Head, Bridlington Bay is rarely too rough for the boats to put out. The fishing parties, especially during the holiday season and at weekends, mostly come from the industrial towns inland, as far away as Leeds and Bradford, with their sights set on cod, haddock, plaice and other smaller flat-fish. The trips last several hours, but by evening most of the boats have returned.

A good place, Bridlington Harbour. 'The rights and property of and in the harbour, the piers, jetties, wharves, offices, and other properties are . . . vested absolutely in the Bridlington Harbour Commissioners'. If you drop litter in the harbour it means a £20 maximum fine. A row of stall-like shops by the entrance to the pier offers a variety of foods – peeled prawns, cockles, shrimps, mussels, whelks, winkles and oysters. An air-sea rescue base still operates from Bridlington. In the 1930s Aircraftsman Shaw was stationed here, and a sundial in the neat South Cliff Gardens overlooking the head of the harbour commemorates him, Lawrence of Arabia.

Bridlington's sea-front skyline contrasts sharply with that of Filey. It has no crescents or elegant terraces, but is a mixture of angles and broken skylines creating their own disordered attraction. In front of them is the huge Floral Pavilion: acres of glass, a cross between a railway station and a greenhouse. Nearby are the clean, hard lines of the new solarium and swimming pool which cannot match the distant textured cliffs of Flamborough. The southern end of the Esplanade yields to Garrison Street, where the raucous voices and glaring lights of bingo halls and fun palaces compete for the valued custom of the visitors who are bored or unmoved by sea and evening sky.

Top: left (9)   early Norman tower of Weaverthorpe church, showing projecting staircase; *right* (10)   Perpendicular tower of Hedon church, for which money was left in 1428. *Bottom* (11)   Wressle Castle, built for Sir Thomas Percy c. 1380.

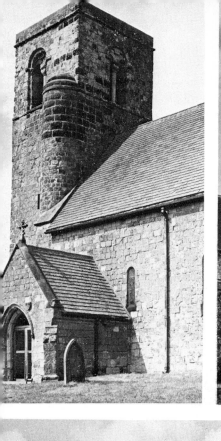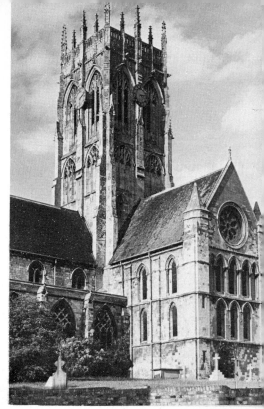

CHAPTER FOUR

Holderness
Bridlington to Spurn

The main road south from Bridlington leaves the coast for a more inland stretch as far as Skipsea. There is a pleasant avenue of young trees for two miles, and farther on a side road leads down to Fraisthorpe, a village of no particular distinction apart from some quite good sands a mile away, with the site of the original village nearby. Barmston also lies off the main road, a very definite 'street' village strung out along the road that leads to the sea. At the end of the road is a slipway for boats, a caravan site, and a rather pebbly beach. The church is at the west end of the village, alone in a field, its walls a mixture of stones and rough cobbles.

Barmston Old Hall is close to the church, but a better view of it can be obtained from the main road. The Boyntons used to live here from Elizabethan times until after the Civil War, when they moved to Burton Agnes, but of their former home only one range remains. The Old Hall, built of mellow brick, and dating mainly from the seventeenth century, is now a farmhouse with transomed two- and three-light windows looking out across the moat, still with water in it.

Holderness is a name which has come down through history: the modern map does not show it – although the *Readers' Digest Atlas of the British Isles* indicates it as stretching southwards from near Bridlington to Spurn Head. The River Hull is its western boundary and Barmston Dyke is recognised as its northern limit. The main road from Bridlington to Driffield

12.   Bempton Cliffs, the northernmost limit of the English chalk, is a nature reserve and the only English mainland breeding-place for gannets.

does not reveal the Holderness character. But as you drive southwards from Bridlington by the Beverley road, the A.165, you definitely leave the chalk and enter the clay. The horizons are lower, the trees more prominent in isolation and the lanes seemingly more winding.

The nature of Holderness was recognised by Chaucer, whose Summoner comments:

> 'Lordinges, ther is in Yorkshire as I gesse,
> A marshy contree called Holdernesse.'

Low-lying marshes still exist, so do the little glacial mounds, the morainic ridges and the slow winding streams. Nowhere does it reach the 100 foot contour. But Chaucer did not know of the copses and woodlands, nor did he realise that the rich soil of Holderness made it one of the main cornlands of the north. Drayton, writing much later, made no bones about it, for his *East Riding* claims:

> 'Rich Holderness I have excelling for grain.'

Historically Holderness dates from the Norman Conquest for William made it a large feudal seigniory, granting its lordship in the first place to one Drogo de Brevere, a Flemish adventurer. An early chronicler of Meaux Abbey records that de Brevere had killed his wife, a relative of the King, but he managed to reach William before the news did. He persuaded the King to grant him a big enough loan to let him flee the country.

You pick up these threads in the warp of Holderness history as you follow the B.1242 to Skipsea where another minor road, the B.1249, leads westwards past the church on its little hill, and crosses the now insignificant Stream Dyke before passing the two or three buildings which comprise Skipsea Brough. An official 'Ancient Monument' sign points the way to the proper 'Skipsea Brough', the huge earthworks which are all that survive of the original motte-and-bailey castle of Drogo de Brevere. The grassy track which leads to the mound is a slightly raised causeway linking the outer ramparts to the motte itself.

These outer ramparts, as high as the motte, form a crescent almost 300 yards long.

Elder and hawthorn grow on the steep sides of the 36 foot high motte, whose plateau-top is 100 feet across. To the north-east evening sunlight picks out the lighthouse on Flamborough Head, while westwards the eye scans the distant gentle slopes of the Wolds. Long shadows are thrown down the rampart slopes, and Skipsea Church is prominent beyond the line of the Stream Dyke. Its nave and chancel show some Norman work suggesting it may have been contemporary with de Brevere's castle. Cobblestone courses show a herring-bone pattern both in the chancel and at the west end of the nave. The nearly circular churchyard hints at a very old establishment, or is merely the result of the lie of the land.

Skipsea village is unpretentious, of the usual brick, eighteenth- and nineteenth-century, but with one older house on the south side of the road, obviously seventeenth-century and claiming Quaker associations. The sands are a safe mile away, but the road to Hornsea turns a right-angle to continue its way parallel to the coast, leaving a new housing estate to point the way to the sea where caravan sites have continued from Ulrome, north-east of Skipsea – the whole extending to two miles. Their summertime population must run into hundreds, maybe thousands, which means a big seasonal increase in trade for the district.

Southwards from Skipsea the road passes prosperous-looking farms with their sheltering trees, ranges of brick buildings and fertile fields. Atwick presents its most attractive aspect to the main road which cuts through the middle of the village spaced round a triangular green with good-looking houses fronting on to it. A stumpy shaft on a base of three high, well-worn steps, is all that survives of the village cross. A lane west of the village leads to the red-brick church of 1876, and nearby is the Holy Well. Once it may have been holy; now it is an untidy, overgrown pond displaying the notice 'Dumping of rubbish prohibited'.

Atwick holds a secret unique in Britain. In 1972 it was chosen as the ideal site for one of the biggest gas-holders in the world.

A mile below the surface is a thick layer of rock salt into which boreholes have been driven. High-pressure water from the North Sea half a mile away, will be forced into the salt to dissolve it, and hence create enormous caverns – six of them, enough to hold 4,000 million cubic feet of North Sea gas, a day's supply for the whole country. The first sea water was scheduled to flow into the salt-beds in autumn 1974, and the job is expected to be completed in 1976.

Hornsea is the main seaside resort between Bridlington and Spurn. Originally a fishing village, it has gone the way of countless others in exchanging fish for folk, and, since early last century, attracting increasing numbers of holiday-makers. In 1835 it was the 'principal watering-place for Hull', although the railway did not reach it until 1864. In the thirteenth century the abbots of York profited from the market they had allowed there; in addition they levied tolls on ships, wrecks, strangers passing through the town, bread and beer, and land tithes. They ensured that these were collected by building a prison, having a pillory, and erecting a gallows. Their rapacious cruelty was obviously one of the least acceptable faces of monasticism. Undoubtedly, the folk of Hornsea must have been relieved when the Dissolution removed such tyranny.

The oldest part of the town lies away from the sea. Market Street curves round into South Gate, with St Nicholas's Church on the corner of Newbigin. The old market cross now stands in the churchyard, and there is the pillar of another old cross further down South Gate, believed to be an old preaching cross erected by an abbot of York.

The church is large, impressive and unusually light, 'nearly all glass' as Pevsner puts it. A crypt beneath the east bay of the chancel is tunnel-vaulted in brick and contains a fireplace in one of its two rooms. This old part of the town has retained much of its character because Hornsea Mere has prevented any westward development. Half a mile to the east, however, there has been the usual attenuated growth, north along Cliff Road, south along the Promenade, without anything much to redeem it. Massive concrete walls have been built to withstand the erosive clawing of the North Sea, and a series of groynes protrude their protective fingers against the southwards motions of waves and tides.

There is an irony about Hornsea's greatest asset. Hornsea Mere, 495 acres in area and five miles round, is the largest freshwater lake in Yorkshire, yet is less than a mile from the sea. Formed by the retreating glacial ice it is characteristic of the marshy type of landscape which occurs in various parts of Holderness, a sort of Norfolk Broads in the East Riding. Its fishing rights were once the cause of a fearful squabble between the Abbot of Meaux and the Abbot of St Mary's, York, who even engaged champions to fight a duel on their behalf, but eventually an obvious compromise was reached – York Abbey fished the north shore, Meaux Abbey the south.

Hornsea Mere is leased to the Royal Society for the Protection of Birds as a nature reserve, but fishing and sailing are allowed, though not the use of motor-boats or canoes. A public footpath allows good access to most of the banks of the lake. A local firm runs the boat-hire side of the Mere's assets very sensibly, and has developed the site at the town end of the lake to cater for visitors who come to watch the coloured sails of the yachts – Fireflies, Ospreys, Swordfish – and to observe the birds, swans, grebes, herons, Canada geese, and teal. They may even fish for roach, tench, perch and pike. Hornsea Mere has multiple uses, and pleases many people, but I like it best in an evening when most of the visitors have left it to the birds and the wind in the reeds. Evening sunlight highlights the church tower, the houses of old Hornsea, and later, as the sun goes down, the colours of its departing are thrown back for extra delight in the rippling waters of the lake.

Many signposts point the way to Hornsea Pottery, a mile south of the town. Another little country pottery, you might think, similar to those in other tourist areas of Britain. No, not this one, for it is something definitely out of the ordinary.

To begin with there is a free park for a thousand cars plus a large field for picnicking. Most other things in the 28-acre leisure complex are also free. Well-signposted paths lead you through beautiful gardens to a small zoo, an aviary, a play-centre for children, a tastefully laid out piazza for relaxation, for having refreshments, for people-watching, for time-passing. There is a restaurant, a splendid garden centre, a lake with water-fowl, and a self-service shop in the pottery centre where good quality 'seconds' can be bought. You are made to feel welcome, and you don't have to spend money. You can also enjoy escorted tours of the factory itself. The garden centre and restaurant are self-supporting, while most of the profit comes from the pottery shop.

Hornsea Pottery was started in 1949 by two brothers, recently out of the army, working in an outhouse in Hornsea with an electric kiln and no knowledge of pottery-making. They have certainly expanded during a quarter of a century, deservedly so, for it is good sense to provide so many amenities free, in such well-planned surroundings. You don't need to pay a king's ransom for happiness, and it is rather fun to hear a mynah bird say 'Hallo' with a Yorkshire accent.

Aldbrough is a large attractive village east of the main road, with broad streets and a particularly good pub for food, the George and Dragon. Further down the road towards Withernsea, Garton lies just to the seaward, a small village of a few farms and cottages, and a church with some good sculptured heads. A mile to the east is Grimston Garth, one of the East Riding's important houses. It is obvious that visitors are not welcomed for there are high fences and numerous warning notices, while the hall itself can be glimpsed only from a distance. It is a pity a closer approach cannot be made, since the house was designed by John Carr and dates from 1781–86. He built it for Thomas Grimston in good Georgian Gothic, in the form of a castellated triangle with three round corner towers, while from the base of the triangle projects another wing. All the buildings are castellated, as is the central, higher hexagonal tower. The stable block is also castellated and the gatehouse, built in 1812 by Thomas Earle, and much nearer to the main road. For its purpose this is an enormous affair, complete with polygonal turrets, battlements and even a portcullis.

Hilston is another small village lying east of the main road. Admiral Storr's Tower crowns a low grassy hill to its north, an octagonal brick structure 50 feet high, built by Mr Justice Storr in 1750 either as a folly or as a landmark to mariners. It has a turret stair at the back, was once used as a cottage, but is now in need of repair, and is apparently inhabited by hens. There were only six houses in Hilston in 1783, three of which were the Admiral's, the Rectory, and the Poorhouse.

Hilston's church is the third on the site. First came a tiny Anglo-Norman building, 19 yards long, six yards wide, cobble-built. It lasted until 1860, and the replacement survived until a German bomb hit it in 1941. For many years a private house was used as a church until, in 1957, the new church was consecrated. Brick, with an impressive west tower surmounted by an attractive cupola, it is very light and spacious inside. Designed by Francis Johnson of Bridlington, it has a most appealing east window by L. C. Evetts of Newcastle. The bell came from the demolished church at Wharram Percy while the original north door of the first church, maintained in Pearson's building for Sir Tatton Sykes, now survives as the south door-way of the present church.

A lonely lane leads down the coast to Tunstall, where another church is built mainly of shore-cobbles. The melancholy of the Holderness coast is very apparent here. The closer that buildings remain to the land's edge, the more sadly they await their eventual collapse. Nothing can resist the inch-and-a-half a week erosion. In 150 years the sea has moved 400 yards towards the church. At this rate, it and the village will have gone within three more centuries. Perhaps the temporary nature of the nearby caravans will give them the last laugh.

Back to the B.1242 it is only a short distance to Roos, where much of the village has migrated northwards from the church, and is now centred round the right-angled bend made by the main road from Hornsea to Withernsea. North and south the houses straggle, with little to commend them, but the church yields its own reward. A stone-flagged path between an avenue of yew shrubs takes you up three separate flights of five steps to the west door. The Victorian porch dates from 1842 when the church was over-restored by the Rector, the Reverend Charles Hotham, exactly four centuries after the tower was built.

But the church's most unusual feature is outside. At its north-east corner is the vestry, formerly a fourteenth-century chantry chapel where masses would have been said for deceased benefactors. In the angle between its south-west corner and the north wall of the church is a circular tower which might possibly have been a watch-tower for the castle of the Barons de Ros. Access to it was by a spiral stairway which led first to the priest's room above the chantry chapel, and then continued a few steps more into the 'watch-tower' turret.

Also seen best from outside is the fourteenth-century brick-work above the clerestory. This is some of the earliest in York-shire outside Hull and Beverley, and its weathered rose-pink colour blends attractively with the harsher tones and textures of the cobbles and rubble used for the rest of the building. The clerestory windows themselves contain fragments of medieval glass. The de Ros is the premier barony of England; the village seems little concerned about it.

Withernsea was a small village in 1851, with just over 100 people. At the time, Anthony Bannister was an alderman in Hull who, perhaps inspired by the enthusiasm of fellow-Yorkshireman George Hudson, promoted a scheme for open-ing up the coast of Holderness by a railway from Hull which would connect many small intermediate villages. Of the coastal villages surveyed, Withernsea was eventually selected as one to be organised for visitors. The Withernsea Pier, Promenade, Gas and General Improvement Company Limited obtained approval to build that essential item of seaside equipment, an iron pier. A local architect, Cuthbert Brodrick, designed the railway station, and the line was formally opened in 1854 with the usual festivities.

The seeds of seaside popularity were sown. In the four months of that summer over 63,000 passengers travelled from Hull to Withernsea. The Station Hotel became the very splen-did Queen's Hotel, 11 bays long and two and a half storeys high, with an iron balcony at the first floor. In 1902, Sir James Reckitt and Francis Reckitt of Hull bought it with its grounds, and presented it to the Hull Royal Infirmary as a convalescent home. The railway itself passed into the hands of the North

Eastern Railway in 1860, and just over a century later ceased to function.

Withernsea Pier enjoyed a much briefer life than the railway which had helped to make it popular. In October 1880, during a severe storm the coal-laden barge *Saffron* sailed clean through it and took away about 200 feet of pier. Repairs were made, but in March 1882 another violent gale removed the rest of the pier. What remains are the impressive stone pier towers, battlemented as a replica of Conway Castle, and serving the dual purpose of Coastguard Station and St John's Ambulance Brigade Headquarters.

The promenade extends north and south from the pier towers; there is the usual entertainment complex, and well-kept gardens. Summer swimmers brave the chilly waves; the sand and shingle shore attracts the families now as they did those of a century ago. A quarter of a mile from the sea-front stands Withernsea lighthouse, a white, tapering octagonal tower, 125 feet high, and sharing with the one at Lowestoft the rare distinction of being a 'keeper and wife' building.

The B.1362 leads inland from Withernsea to Hedon, passing Batty's Corner and Bunker's Hill before reaching Halsham. Here lived the Holderness Constables from the twelfth century until the seventeenth century. Their house has long since gone, but the church in which they were buried stands sheltered by tall trees a little way from the road. Its greatest glory is in the chancel where the grouping of finely sculptured sedilia and piscina reveals a quite spectacular decoration of five centuries ago. The stone chair may be a surviving Frid Stool, although there is some doubt about this claim. There is a delicately canopied alabaster tomb, possibly of Sir John Constable, 1407, and his wife, but the remaining Constables were duly collected and re-interred in the Constable Mausoleum across the road. Designed by Thomas Atkinson, and built 1792–1802, this is an elegant, circular temple, domed, with blank arches and blank panels above. By the roadside the brick building with stepped gables of the former Free School at Halsham, founded by a Constable in 1584, is now a private house.

Burton Pidsea and Burstwick are the only other villages of note before Hedon is reached. Holderness was once governed from Burstwick, presumably from the castle whose moat only can now be identified a mile north-west of the village, near Hall Garth. Both Edward I and Edward II are said to have lived there, and the wife of Robert Bruce was once imprisoned in the castle. In the village itself the church has the Royal Arms of Charles I on a board beneath an arch of the north arcade, and its reverse side has a painting showing the execution of the King. The initials of John Catlyn, the then vicar, who placed the painting in the church in 1676, accompany an inscription in Latin.

Returning to the coast, the main road from Withernsea to Spurn Head cuts inland to Patrington, but a narrow, unclassified road keeps much closer to the coast. It branches off the A.1033 at Hollym, an unpretentious village whose church has a west tower of yellow brick, with the rest of it having the yellow broken by bands of red masonry. The interior is almost clinically clean, far pleasanter in appearance than the outside, and in the churchyard is a group of low headstones with good lettering of the early eighteenth century.

Holmpton shows a large-scale display of radio apparatus, another church of yellow and red brick, and a farm nearby called Trinity House Farm. Right-angled corners take the road zig-zag fashion down the coast. At one point near Dimlington it is only a few feet from the edge of the low cliffs. As a result it has become one more dumping-ground for a wide variety of rubbish. Those responsible for this unnecessary addition to an unimpressive scene are aware that coastal erosion will soon devour the garbage and junk, but even the sea will find it hard to digest the plastic bags and metal containers.

Eventually the minor road reaches Easington and the B.1445 from Patrington, which here ceases to be classified. The sea is half a mile away to the east, the Humber just over a mile to the south-west. It is a place of sea breezes, and an altogether clean, friendly appearance. The church tower rises above the pantiled roofs of the village, which has a broad, open street to the east, a narrow winding one to the south. Buttresses are stepped up to the battlements; from the tower arch a grotesque known as the 'Easington Imp' looks down, and medieval gravestones serve as lintels for two windows in the north aisle.

Much of the church, as well as many cottage walls, and boundary walls of fields near the village, are made of rounded cobbles from the shore, in a herring-bone pattern. A small barn near the church shows this very well, but is rather over-shadowed by a fine brick tithe-barn close by. This has a newly-thatched roof, and from its western wall a brick-built gin-gang projects, its pantiled roof supported on fine timber beams and rafters.

Easington has an unusual, modern claim to fame, being the first English terminal of North Sea gas, which is brought here by a single 36-inch pipe from a source over 40 miles out to sea. The installations are east of the village, a network of pipes, pylons and girders. More elegant, though with a more melancholy history, is a stone pillar adjoining a house by the road to Kilnsea. Its stones are thought to have come from a church now beneath the waves. There is a boulder of Shap granite by it.

Kilnsea is two miles away, and the road crosses a seawall on the way. Yorkshire's most easterly village is thus isolated from the rest of the county. It was once a fishing town with cliffs, but its continuing fate has been to suffer from the eroding grasps of the North Sea. Its serried ranks of caravans to the north only emphasise the transitory nature of its life. The human migrants seek them in the summer; in the winter months they stand forlorn and sad. Melancholy seems to pervade. In 1822 only thirty houses remained with the church. In 1831 half of the church together with the tower, went over the cliff, to be followed 19 years later by the remains of the building. At the end of the century, when members of the East Riding Antiquarian Society came to see what was left of the church they had to wait for a very low tide indeed. When this occurred, they stood on the low cliffs and gazed seawards. The ruins of the church were 250 yards out to sea; only the font was saved, and this is now in the new church, built of red and yellow brick in 1864.

A café, once a pub called The Bluebell, has a plaque recording that it was built in 1847 when it was 534 yards from the sea.

Now it is less than half that distance. Not even the badly-built sea defences are secure against the attack of the North Sea. Built during the 1914–18 war to protect the gun emplacements, the broken masses of concrete lie shattered and untidy on the beach at Kilnsea, not far from the Coastguard Station transferred there from Spurn Head.

The peninsula of Spurn juts appendix-like into the Humber for nearly four miles. Its 280 acres of land above the high-water mark, plus 477 acres below it, have been owned as a nature reserve since 1960 by the Yorkshire Naturalists' Trust, to secure it as an important resting-place on the migration routes of many species of birds. The public road from Kilnsea ends at the northern neck of the reserve, but a toll road continues along it as far as the lighthouse. For 30 pence you can drive down the narrow concrete track, which has passing-places, but you cannot take a dog with you, on or off a lead, in or out of a car. There is no toll paid if you walk along the peninsula, and though this obviously takes longer, it is far more rewarding.

Stevenson's dictum that 'it is better to travel hopefully than to arrive' is very appropriate to Spurn, for the worst part is at the southern tip. By Warren Cottage and the Bird Observatory at the entrance, the peninsula is flat and relatively wide, but it soon tapers to a neck of slightly higher land between 50 and 100 yards wide. For me, this is the best part of Spurn, particularly at high water when so little land separates the surging North Sea from the shallow, muddy waters of the Humber across the Kilnsea Clays to the west.

'Narrow Neck', as it is called, has had the artificial protection of groynes and revetments on its eastern side since 1860. Correspondingly, chalk boulders have pitched and accreted on the estuary shore. Previously, Narrow Neck was even lower, so that waves frequently swept over it. In 1915 it was raised on an embankment to carry a railway line to supply the military fort at Spurn Point. For many years, until the present road was constructed, this line was the only land connection to the lighthouse and the lifeboat cottages, and if the wind was right, the men used to sail along on a rail-trolley with a sail – an early form of land-yachting, no doubt. The line is still visible in sections where the road now crosses it.

Marram grass, lyme grass, sea rocket, sea holly and the widely-spread sea buckthorn clothe the sand dunes which extend on either side of the road. The motorist finds vision restricted, and only at occasional places does he see the waters on either side. The walker takes the journey more leisurely, wanders off to the shore-lines, or sits on the turf of the older dunes watching the birds.

South of Narrow Neck, the peninsula widens again irregularly, culminating in a slightly bulbous end where the lighthouse and lifeboat station are situated. The nearer you approach the tip of Spurn the more untidy and derelict does the scene become. Motorists can park their vehicles near the centre of the dereliction, and walk the last few hundred yards. The 120 feet high lighthouse was built in 1895 superseding the 1852 structure which in turn replaced Smeaton's building of 1776. The circular compound with light-keepers' houses associated with Smeaton's lighthouse is still recognisable. The stumpy remains of the 1852 lighthouse still stand on the estuary side of the point, to the north of the gloomy black-tarred row of lifeboat-men's cottages. The only full-time professional lifeboat crew in Britain live in this row of cottages, the Royal National Lifeboat Institute regarding the station of such importance as to justify this. If you walk down by the end of the cottages, and work your way down the Humber side of the tip of Spurn to the very end you can appreciate the significance of the R.N.L.I.'s decision. The tide-race in and out of the Humber around Spurn can reach seven knots; currents are muddily treacherous, especially out at Stony Binks, a few hundred yards offshore.

The westward-curving finger of Spurn beckons ships into the broad sweep of the Humber. Trawlers return from their cold and distant fishing grounds, and the bigger vessels glide smoothly into the estuary, or ride at anchor between the arms of Yorkshire and Lincolnshire awaiting the next high tide. Half a mile to the south the Bull Lightship stands watch and ward on her uneasy anchors, while her sister, the Spurn Lightship, holds a lonelier vigil five miles away to the east. Somewhere between them, beneath the waves, but most likely not so very far from the present seaward shore, two towns lie buried.

Spurn has a long recorded history. About 1,300 years ago a small monastery was established on the promontory. It is possible that Danes landed there in 867, set up their raven standard, and founded Ravenser, or Ravensburg, on the narrow spit of sand and shingle that was the Spurn of those days. Early in the thirteenth century a new spit of land appeared, and this was called Ravenserodd, meaning 'the headland near Ravenser'. By then, the original settlement was more firmly established near the northern end of the peninsula, but by about 1235 the small new town and port of Ravenserodd was developing. Within a few years quays had been built; in 1251, market rights and a fair were granted to Ravenserodd, and a church and chapel added 20 years later.

Ravenser, too, had acquired borough status by about 1300, having greater wealth and importance even than Hull itself, and returning two members to Parliament, and ships to the navy.

In 1332, Baliol embarked from Ravenser to attack the Scots, but within a decade the work of the sea was hazarding the two towns, and in 1355 bodies were being washed out of the graveyard. Two years later, the sea regularly inundated Ravenserodd, and by 1360 most of the merchants of both towns had left for the safer havens of Hull and Grimsby. In the following year, Ravenserodd was 'totally annihilated by the floods of the Humber and the inundations of the Great Sea', a visitation blamed by the Abbot of Meaux on the wickedness and piracies of the town's inhabitants. By the end of the century nothing was left of the two towns.

Spurn is made by the sea. Equally it can be destroyed by it. Currents and tides of sea and river shift the unstable sand and shingle. Perhaps if the sea again severed Spurn from the mainland, it would once more disappear, to be returned a few decades later, some distance to the west. This happened when Ravenser and Ravenserodd died. Within 30 years there was a hermitage on a new spit of land, and in 1538 Leland names Ravenspurn on his itinerary.

CHAPTER FIVE

Holderness

The Hull Valley

Returning from Spurn into Holderness is rather like leaving an island for the mainland again. It is some little while before the solitudes of sea and sky are left, but by Easington the land assumes priority again. Skeffling is a small village lying south of the road, with thatched cottages, tall trees, a church in the fields at the end of the village and with the cobbles in its walls a reminder that the estuary is but half a mile away.

At Welwick the main road swings through a corner by the church, passing an attractive grouping of houses, but to the west beckons the slender spire of Patrington's lovely church. Not without good reason is it called the 'Queen of Holderness', and justifiably merits praise from Pevsner: 'For sheer architectural beauty few parish churches in England can vie with Patrington'.

From the back lane which cuts across the south of Patrington the view opens up to reveal the church and its spire with the village cricket field making a perfect foreground setting. On a summer Saturday this is as English a scene as a man may hope to see.

But what is so splendid about Patrington that attracts the superlatives? The same, perhaps, as that which Salisbury has, grace, elegance, the calm, cool beauty of carved stone, but above all unity in design. Patrington church was built in a short space of time, most of it during the 40 years before the Black Death in 1348. Patrington's weathercock is 189 feet above the ground, the spire rising above the tower from behind an octagonal screen of panels, two to each face, with pinnacles above, adorning the tower like a crown. The slender beauty of a soaring spire needs a flat landscape from which its sky-seeking accent draws the eye, taking it, as it were, from earth to heaven. All the stranger is it, therefore, to find that, apart from the open view already described, Patrington's church is far less easily seen from the village itself.

Cruciform in plan, the church is 141 feet long and 86 feet wide at its transepts. Detailed carving on the outside is matched by a beautiful unity inside the building. The double aisles to the nave and transepts emphasise the soaring lines of Decorated grace, and in the window tracery the poetry of stone progresses, geometric in the transepts, curvilinear in the nave, to Perpendicular in the east window.

Apart from the church, Patrington is a pleasant village of a few streets intersecting at right angles, with plenty of eighteenth- and nineteenth-century houses, and a handsome Methodist church of 1811 with a clean Classical front.

A road leads south from Patrington towards the flattest landscape in Yorkshire. Sunk Island is a parish created in 1831, the outcome of centuries of reclamation of siltlands from the Humber. Today, no part of Sunk Island is more than 15 feet above sea level; large rectangular fields, flanked by drains, grow fine cereal crops. Hedgerow elms stand sentinel against the low skyline, and the few scattered farms have names as uncompromising as the sombre scenery – East Bank, Stone Creek, Channel, White House, West, Newlands and Outstray – each established over 100 years ago, though some may well have occupied sites used centuries earlier.

As long ago as the tenth century, silt was beginning to accumulate between the Humber's main channel and its northern shoreline, where four streams flowed from south Holderness into the Humber creating deltas colonised between the tides by salt-marsh plants. During the eleventh and twelfth centuries it was possible to build embankments on the higher parts of the silt. Slowly, these helped more tide-free land to be formed, so that a three-mile strip was added to the Humber

13. The south front of Sledmere House, built by Sir Christopher Sykes 1781–8, probably influenced by Wyatt.

coast of Holderness. The streams continued to flow in channels through the silt, and it seems likely that simple sluices were built to hold back the tidal water. In early medieval times some of the newly formed land was ploughed, but most of it remained as sheep pastures.

A great storm occurred in 1256, and in the following three centuries much of the silt lands were lost to the sea, but by the late sixteenth century most of the land losses had ceased. In 1660 embankments between four and six feet high existed on the Humber shoreline, protected on the east by breakwaters. These banks curved inland where the four streams entered the Humber, and tidal sluices were so placed some way upstream from the estuary that they were not damaged by storm waves. Thus were formed tidal channels below the sluices, or clows, providing havens for ships using the Humber, and reaching them along the North Channel, a deep-water channel on the Holderness side, extending from Paull almost to Spurn. Patrington Haven and Hedon Haven were the most important havens, but now the Humber is far away from these places.

By the end of the century the Cherry Cobb and Sunk Sands had so increased in height, that salt-marsh plants were once more flourishing, trapping even more silt so that the higher parts were covered by tides only once or twice a month. Indeed, in 1695, 13 acres of Sunk Sands were embanked to create the nucleus of Sunk Island, and the havens were beginning to silt up.

By 1742 the sands covered about 2,000 acres, and extended for a length of two miles. William Constable, of Burton Constable, initiated serious attempts at draining the sands of Cherry Cobb and Sunk Island. The work was completed in 1770. Sunk Island continued to grow westwards so that by 1800 the two islands were joined by sandbanks and mudflats, and in 1831 the new parish of Sunk Island was created as part of the Holderness mainland – 6,000 acres of rich soil, well-drained and full of promise.

Sunk Island is a Crown estate. Some of its 15 farms, as well as many of the cottages, carry a 'V.R.' monogram, and often a

Top: left (14) Flamborough Lighthouse, built 1674; *right* (15) Anglo-Saxon cross at Nunburnholme dating from c. 1000. *Bottom* (16) The ruined church at Wharram Percy, showing Norman tower and south arcade.

crown, on their front walls, together with a date, usually in the 1850s when most of the building was carried out. The familiar red brick of Holderness was used together with slate for the roofs. Some of the houses have strange gables, one pair of cottages near the church seems to be an early 'semi-detached', and the very plain church was built in 1877.

No road runs eastwards or westwards from Sunk Island. The Winestead Drain and the Keyingham Drain, cut in the late eighteenth century, are not bridged in their lower sections. So Sunk Island is still, in a way, an island, where the roads go through right-angled bends characteristic of a late-enclosed landscape. There is a fenland quality about its low horizons and fertile soil, but the absence of church towers or spires contributes to a feeling of melancholy, for without them is less reason to lift up the eyes. However, the road that leads to Ottringham has recently had some trees planted along both sides, sycamores mostly, so eventually there will be an avenue, a windbreak, and a contrast in the skyline.

West of Patrington the main road swings through two right-angles and passes the end of Winestead's single street of houses, and, a field's distance from the road, Winestead church. Standing in a clump of elms, the tower-less church has rounded cobbles in its walls, and is much bigger inside than I expected it to be. Temple Moore restored it in 1893. The Hildyard Chapel is very early seventeenth-century, with good wall plaques to various members of the family, but the dominant feature is the armoured figure of Sir Christopher Hildyard, 1602, lying on a half-rolled-up mattress, with elaborate heraldry and carving around him, and a cock, the Hildyard crest, at his feet.

In 1614 the Hildyards presented the living to Andrew Marvell senior, who later gained preferment to Hull. While he was at Winestead his son Andrew was born in 1621. Subsequently educated at Hull and Cambridge, he travelled widely in Europe during our own Civil Wars. In 1657 he became assistant to Milton, and from 1659 until his death in 1678 he represented the Hull electors in Parliament. Most of Andrew Marvell's best lyric poetry was written before his parliamentary career began.

and reflected a genuine appreciation of natural beauty and of gardens.

Ottringham, the next village along the Hull road, is grouped around its proud-spired church. Not so splendid as Patrington's, it nevertheless has a tower arch with good Norman zigzag decoration carefully adjusted to create a pointed arch. Perhaps the strangest feature is the lectern, simply a stone in the north wall of the chancel shaped to take a book. The railway line from Hull to Withernsea passed a mile to the north of the village, and another smaller settlement grew up around the station.

Keyingham, like Ottringham, shows the evidence in its name of early English settlement, dating probably from the late fifth or early sixth centuries. A very low ridge was sufficient encouragement to establish a base which, over the centuries has gradually expanded into a large though compact village whose street pattern is almost of gridiron planning. Probably once of greater market importance than it is now, Keyingham has three crosses, or their remains, and a church which required the addition of two aisles in the thirteenth century, presumably to accommodate a growing population. In the church is an old hourglass in its iron stand, and a wall tablet to John Angel, benefactor of local lighthouses.

Hedon is one of England's oldest boroughs, whose first charter goes back to 1170. A second charter was obtained from King John in 1200, and by 1272 a charter for an eight-day fair in August had been granted by Henry III, additional privileges ensuing with a longer charter in 1348. But long before then its importance as a commercial port on the Humber had already passed to Hull, and Hedon's long decline was under way.

Approach it from any direction and Hedon is dominated by the magnificent tower of St Augustine's Church – 'The King of Holderness', as it has long been known. The building was started when Hedon's prosperity was great, at the end of the twelfth century, but most of the exterior is characteristic Early English. Nave and aisles are early fourteenth-century in their pointed purity, and there is a large Perpendicular west window. Street was responsible for the restoration 100 years ago, and rebuilt the south transept with its rose window and lancets below. But it is the tower which gives to Hedon's church the apparent dignity and grandeur of a small cathedral. Its cost was met by a subsidy being levied on the burgesses of Hedon in 1428. They must have paid up well, for the resultant crossing-tower stands with pierced parapet and 16 proud pinnacles, a 130-foot landmark for miles around.

The old centre of the town today lies north from the main Hull–Patrington road where the Market Place is a widening of the street east of the church. Walk round the gridiron pattern of streets, the typical planned layout of a new town of the twelfth century, and notice how the street names have the sound of past centuries about them – Souttergate, Churchgate, Magdalen Gate, St Augustinegate, and Fletchergate – still quite narrow, with mainly eighteenth- and nineteenth-century buildings, but nothing very grand. The best bit of Hedon, where its history seems most clear, is in Market Hill, an open triangle of ground, now partly grassed, where the old Wednesday and Saturday markets were held. Larger, more elegant houses border this area, but the ancient market rights have ensured its not being built over.

Three artificial harbours or havens were created south of the town, each oriented north-south, so that they were parallel to some of the streets. The River Hedon made one of them: west of it the West Haven was dug, while the Humbleton Beck to the east was deepened to make the harbour called The Fleet. Later, as the town grew eastwards, a fourth haven was built. By 1200 Hedon had more than a mile of quays, but in another 100 years it was declining. Yet Hedon added two more parish churches, St James's and St Nicholas's, and the fourteenth-century population exceeded 1,000. By 1550 both the additional churches had gone, and in 1536 Leland wrote that 'se crekes parting aboute the saide Town did insulate it, and Shippis lay aboute the Town: but now men come to it by 3 Bridges . . . sum Places where the Shippis lay be overgrowen with Flagges and Reades, and the Haven is very sorely decay'd'.

The streets of Hedon have a rather wistful quietness about them, but I must admit to not having seen Hedon on a market day. However, it can boast, in the old Town Hall, what is possibly the oldest civic mace in England, a beautifully decorated object just over two feet long, and bearing a crown with the royal arms of England and France. It is said to date from Henry V's time. Ironically, another historical survival in Hedon is the very elegant stone cross, called the Kilnsea Cross, which was washed up on the coast there in 1818. The story is that it was originally erected at Ravenser, on Spurn in 1399 to mark the place where Bolingbroke landed in his attempt to claim the throne. The 20 foot high, very worn cross, now stands in the garden of Holyrood House in Baxtergate, an old people's home.

Paull is two miles south-west of Hedon, at the edge of the Humber. Once a fishing village it now looks up-river to the works, wharves, and docks of Salt End, Marfleet and Hull. The little lighthouse of 1836 has an upper balcony and a house adjoining, but its light no longer gleams. An early fifteenth-century church stands rather aloof in the fields to the east of the village, while a mile beyond that is Paull Holme Tower, now ruined, but formerly a fifteenth-century tower-house of brick with a tunnel-vaulted basement, very much in the style of the peel-towers of the Border Country.

The road which leaves Hedon on the north passes the site of the railway station. A brick building by the roadside was the station goods-shed built when the railway came in 1854. Its positioning reflects an unusual effect of the old medieval rights of Hedon, for it lies just outside the old borough boundary, the rest of the station being inside. Part of the old privileges allowed the borough to take tolls on all goods unloaded within its bounds. Obviously, the Hull and Withernsea Railway Company would not wish to pay such tolls on goods they handled at Hedon, so they built the goods-shed outside the town boundary.

Preston village retains many attractive houses of the eighteenth and nineteenth centuries, together with a church with a good tower. Its nearness to Hull makes it an obvious choice for commuters who like to have a green belt between them and their place of work. A similar way of life is arising at Sproatley, the next village three miles to the north, where more trees and the semblance of a green are perhaps a hint of the proximity of Burton Constable Hall.

There are two approaches to this splendid house; the 'back door' one by the Old Lodge and the lake, now a well-organised caravan park and outdoor leisure area, and the more formal and impressive one from the east, along Ellerby Lane.

The Constables are believed to have come over at the time of the Norman Conquest, and it is likely that Drogo de Brevere granted the family lands in Holderness. Certainly they lived at Halsham, site of the Constable Mausoleum already referred to, but they had also acquired the manor of Burton in the early part of the twelfth century, and in the sixteenth century the family moved there from Halsham, and the first Tudor hall was built.

Of the many generations of Constables, it is to two in particular that the present building and its grounds owe their origins. Cuthbert Tunstall, a distant relative, acquired the estate in 1718, when he himself was 40, and took the name of Constable. His son, William, was born at Burton Constable in 1721, and was fortunate enough to inherit many of his father's artistic and intellectual interests, as well as a deep love of the contrasting fields of science and botany. Both men contributed a great deal to the Burton Constable of today.

The original Tudor house was most likely built by Sir Henry Constable, who died in 1606. Then it was a characteristic Elizabethan building with an east front one storey lower than it is now. Cuthbert Constable had started the re-designing and refurnishing in the 1730s, which were completed during William's day, in 1778. Many of the original plans for the alterations are now on display in the Muniment Room, and these show that various architects had been approached for their ideas: Robert Adam, James Wyatt, Thomas Lightoller, Thomas Atkinson and John Carr of York. Originally the façade was only two storeys, when built around 1600–10, but a third was added in 1759–60, together with a central pediment with a huge coat-of-arms beneath it.

The layout of the park owes more probably to Thomas White, a professional garden-designer, than to Capability Brown who was also approached for plans. Cattle grazed peacefully in the parkland, as I walked on to the five-arched bridge which spans a neck of the lake, producing a narrower stretch to the north, a wider area to the south. This latter part of the lake was gay with the coloured sails of small yachts, and the laughter of youngsters in canoes and rowing boats. The field beyond the lakes was in one part the caravan park, and in the other a caravan and camping site, popular with families with young children. The swans, mallard, greylag geese, and other water-fowl on the lakes are probably the best fed in Yorkshire. There are some who would no doubt throw up their hands in horror at this almost garish desecration of an eighteenth-century parkland and its lakes. I am not of their number. In the past, the Hall itself would have been a centre for culture, for sport, for entertainment. Those days have gone, but the present owner of Burton Constable Hall, John Chichester-Constable, takes the view that some of his 250 acres of beautiful parkland should bring pleasure to many people as well as adding to his own income. So he opened it as a Country Park in 1972, with special facilities for fishing, boating and camping. A large carpark was provided, together with better amenities for the existing caravan park. Closer to the house is a model railway, a children's playground and a zoo, plus duck lawns and aviaries. These are all of much more interest to the many children who accompany their parents to Burton Constable than the usual walk round the house. Lightoller's Stable Block of 1767 now houses various museums, including a collection of old carriages, old motorcycles and cars, and a display of agricultural implements.

As you travel from Burton Constable towards the River Hull, it is sometimes difficult to realise that until relatively recent times, large areas of the valley were inundated for several months of the year. The River Hull drained the eastward side of the Wolds, as well as the boulder clays of Holderness, and was originally much more meandering than it is now. It was also undredged and tidal, so that its land water was frequently ponded back up-river during high tides, so that much valley land was seasonably flooded, resulting in the familar 'carrs'.

A quiet, narrow lane leaves Sproatley, passes the Old Lodge, designed by Wyatt in 1786 in the form of a four-centred arch with two turrets and lower wings, and winds along the west side of the grounds. At Coniston, it meets the main Hull–Bridlington road, but before following it northwards, carry on straight across to Swine. This is literally a dead-end village along a single street, with the church at its western end. Beyond that are only tracks to the low-lying farms in the drained silt lands towards the Holderness Drain.

There was once an important pig market here, an aspect of history recognised by the village post office which has a sign depicting a pig hanging by the front gate. There is nothing of outstanding architectural interest in this village of quietly attractive eighteenth- and nineteenth-century brick cottages until you reach the church, splendidly dominant, and telling of a greater glory in times past. Inside it is large and light, with a fine spacious feeling helped by the enormous seven-light east window of clear glass. The nave, dating from 1150, was originally the chancel of a fine priory church, whose former west end now lies buried beneath a farmhouse. The aisles were added around 1170, and the present eighteenth-century tower replaced an even earlier one. A very beautiful sixteenth-century screen, with linenfold panelling, tracery and badges of the Davey, Hilton, Melton and Lascelles families separates the north aisle from the Hilton Chapel. There, in the grey coolness of mutilated alabaster, lie three Hilton knights in fourteenth-century armour, two of them with their ladies.

Other groups help to create in Swine the finest set of effigies of any East Riding village church. The two small sets of choir-stalls have some jolly little misericords, mainly heads, and one of a man looking upside-down between his legs.

The priory for Cistercian nuns was founded at Swine in 1150. However, when Archbishop Gifford visited it in 1267–8 he was rather amazed to find monks living on the premises, and the lord of the manor paying far too much attention to the nuns! Worse than that, the sick were not being properly cared for, and the prioress was showing favouritism. Things were no better during the next century, when at least two cases were reported of nuns' immorality, one concerning a man from the village, the other, two monks from Meaux Abbey a few miles away. No doubt some very severe punishments were meted out. When the community was dissolved in 1539 it consisted of a prioress and 19 nuns, and apart from the church all that survives is a few grass-covered mounds in the field to the west.

South Skirlaugh is on the main road two miles north of Swine. Walter Skirlaw was born here, later becoming in turn bishop of Lichfield, Wells and Durham. He gave money for the building of St Augustine's Church, 1401–3, a fine Perpendicular unity with nave and chancel in one, the Bishop conceivably thinking of it as a collegiate chapel. Buttressed, pinnacled, embattled, it stands just away from the main road. At the northern end of the village is the old Workhouse, Rowton Villas, dating from 1838. Inevitably of brick, with a seven-bay centre section standing higher than the flanking wings of five bays, until recently it was used as Rural District Council offices.

By branching off westwards, you can follow a narrow lane to Benningholme Hall, a late Georgian house of grey brick, and then past Benningholme Grange you cross the Monk Drain, to Wawne Common and the site of Meaux Abbey. A few mounds and ditches in a field near the road are all that remain above ground of this Cistercian Abbey founded by William le Grosse in 1150. William, the Earl of Albemarle, was too fat to carry out his expected duty of going on a crusade, so he compromised by accepting a suggestion that he founded an abbey. Thus, on the first day of January, 1150, twelve monks came to these low-lying meadows and marshes, damp in the grey mists of a Yorkshire winter, and set up some mud huts, with Adam their abbot. Things became too difficult for Adam, so he moved away to Watton as an anchorite, and was succeeded by Philip, who soon organised the building of a church similar to that at Rievaulx. Within 30 years, the third abbot, William, had dismantled Philip's church, and rebuilt in Early English style. This church was finished in 1253, but a hundred years later was struck by lightning and damaged by fire. During Abbot Thomas's time, the abbey went bankrupt, and for a while the monks had to leave. The Black Death of 1349 reduced the number of monks from 49 to seven, but the survivors stayed on. The abbey later regained its importance to such an extent that when it was dissolved in 1539 it had an abbot, a prior and 23 monks.

Meaux Abbey held many lands in south Holderness, and was responsible for carrying out some of the early drainage schemes. Numerous cuts across the carrs connected their various outlying granges with the River Hull, so that the produce of the dryer lands could be transported by water. Obviously, many of these cuts became useful drainage channels long after they had outlived their original functions, and no doubt the name Monk Drain originated during the monastic importance of Meaux Abbey. A building near the site of the abbey houses some architectural fragments, including two tombstones of fifteenth-century date, and some coloured tiles.

Beyond Meaux, the lane winds northwards to Routh, and the main Beverley road. A right turn, and in less than two miles you are rejoining the A.165 at White Cross, where a very elegant turnpike house, or lodge, looks out on to the roundabout where stand the stumpy remains of an ancient cross, painted white. A mile to the north is Leven, where another road comes in from Hornsea. The New Inn is an elegant building of three bays and a Tuscan porch, and nearby, rather hidden by trees, is a similar house, more recently embellished by the addition of a fine Georgian doorway from a house in Hull. Canal House, as it is called, was built by a widow, Mrs Charlotte Bethell, about 1802. She also built the Leven Canal.

This is a good example of an individual promoting the construction of a small private waterway. Her family had owned a lot of land around Leven, and she wished to increase both its capital value and its rental, by providing a direct link with the River Hull, and hence the Humber, for the export of agricultural produce and the import of building stone, coal and lime. Mrs Bethell's canal was cut westwards from Leven to the River Hull, like a great drain. At its junction with the river was a lock big enough to admit a Yorkshire keel, and having double pairs of gates, since the tidal River Hull was sometimes higher, sometimes lower, than the canal itself. Opened in 1805, the Leven Canal never flourished, but lasted as a navigable way until 1936, being in the same ownership all the time. A footpath leads from the side of the New Inn, to a small, weedy, muddy basin now cut off from the canal by a turf bank, beyond which is the towpath as far as Leven lock, now sealed, although the canal still has plenty of water in it encouraging fishermen. An accommodation bridge at Little Leven permits nothing larger than a rowing-boat beneath it.

Brandesburton, the next village to the north, has a pleasant grouping of houses near the small green, where the shaft and broken head of the village cross stands on a plinth of patched steps. There is a late Norman priest's doorway in the church, and nearby are the schools, red-brick, six-bay buildings with an inscription recording that they were erected in 1843 by the Lord Mayor and Aldermen of London, Governors of Emanuel Hospital. Happily, they are still in use.

By the 1840s the unenclosed pastures of Brandesburton were the biggest commons east of the Wolds, and were not reclaimed as ploughland until 1847. Then, 500 acres of Brandesburton Moor, and 840 acres of carrs were divided into fields of just under 10 acres, tile-drained, fenced with post-and-rail and some quickset hedges, and cultivated. Now a century and a quarter later, the land is rich and fertile. The names of the farms lying just off the road north from Brandesburton date them as of the time of the enclosures, as well as linking them to the landscape they serve: Moor Edge, Moortown, Moorside Farm, Moor Cottage, Moor House and Moor Grange.

North Frodingham lies to the west of the main road, on the B.1249 that runs across the north of Holderness from Skipsea to Great Driffield. The name suggests an early settlement, a fact underlined by the existence of the head of an old Saxon cross found early this century, and now on a window-sill in the church. This has a rare English dedication to St Elgin, and stands on a knoll, half a mile west of the village overlooking the Frodingham Beck, which is a continuation of the Kelk Beck, natural waterways rather than cut drains. The top section of the church-tower was built by Temple Moore for Sir Tatton Sykes in 1892, and low down on its north-west corner buttress there is a stone placed there on 15 September 1815, by which the correct height of water at Frodingham Bridge could be measured.

North Frodingham extends along both sides of a single main street for about a mile, with the remains of an old market cross, its shaft encased in wood, at a road junction. From North Frodingham the road back to Skipsea crosses the main Bridlington road at Beeford, another street village which is expanding at the crossroads. There is some good modern in-filling between groups of eighteenth- and nineteenth-century brick houses – one of these latter, near the school, having a whimsically twisted brick chimney. The church lies north of the village, pleasantly framed against a backcloth of ash and oak, its handsome Perpendicular tower crowned by a delicate parapet, with eight pinnacles soaring above it. From Beeford the A.165 will take us quickly back to Bridlington where our tour of Holderness had begun.

CHAPTER SIX

Bridlington to Great Driffield

A minor road goes westward from Bridlington, roughly following the gentle valley of the elusive Gypsey Race. Boynton is the first village, reached down a wooded lane with white cottages on one side, and ending by the church at the entrance to Boynton Hall which can be seen through the beeches and sycamores of its park. The church looks unpromising from the outside, but the interior provides a happy surprise. Where a crossing tower would normally be, between nave and chancel, two pairs of pillars support a decorated ceiling with a frieze all round. Wrought iron railings surround the bases of the columns and this Georgian elegance results from a rebuilding of most of the church in 1768–70. A tiny organ occupies a small north transept, and the chancel has the altar placed centrally in it, surrounded by walls full of monuments and memorials, mainly commemorating members of the Strickland family from 1673. Beneath the tower at the west end of the church is their family pew, reached by a flight of stairs.

Another connection with the Stricklands is the carved lectern showing 'a turkey in its pride proper'. This crest and the coat-of-arms beneath were granted in 1550 to William Strickland, who commanded one of Cabot's ships in an expedition to South America, and brought back the first turkeys to Britain over 400 years ago.

Boynton Hall was the home of the Stricklands, William (died 1598) being the one who started the building, whose north entrance originally had two wings projecting. Around 1770

85

the space between was filled in, leaving the Tudor wings still projecting on the south. Boynton Hall is now occupied as flats, and a good view of the building can be obtained by walking through the farmyard, reached by the lane which keeps to the right of the entrance pillars of the park. This goes through a small wood, crosses the Gypsey Race, and enters the farmyard. The parkland rises gently to the south, and from a corner by a gate you can look back to the garden front of Boynton Hall, formal and with a gazebo in one corner.

While the improvements were being made to the house, the estate was not being neglected. The Stricklands planted trees not only for pleasure but for profit, creating parklands of economic value, and visual delight, as well as clothing with woodland the slopes of many little valleys in the Wolds. Now some of the timber on the Boynton estates has been felled, and some of the parkland is under plough. I tried to follow a public right-of-way southwards to Carnaby but standing corn defeated me, so I found an alternative track across the hillside to Carnaby Temple, a tower built by Sir William Strickland about 1770. Like so many eighteenth-century follies, it has become derelict. Octagonal, brick, and two storeys high, it still manages to retain its lantern roof, but windows and doors are broken and the masonry is crumbling. It will not be long before Carnaby Temple becomes a memory on a quiet hilltop. Few preservation societies are interested in follies but perhaps some group of eccentric enthusiasts might investigate a Society for the Protection of Obsolete Follies (SPOOF for short!). I returned to Boynton a different way, partly along the Wold Gate, now a metalled lane, but formerly one of the old east-west routes across the Wolds.

Rudston is the next village, two miles west of Boynton, and it also stands on the line of the old Roman road from York to Bridlington. This large, friendly village has a number of claims to fame. A prehistoric monolith, a Roman villa and tesselated pavements, the Gypsey Race, Winifred Holtby, and Sir Alexander MacDonald of the Isles – each in turn has played a part in its history.

The church at Rudston is on a hill towards the east of the

rather dispersed village, with the huge monolith only a few feet from its north-east corner. The name of the village derives from the 'rood' and 'stan', old English for 'cross' and 'stone'. It has been suggested that the 'rood' part of the name may indicate that at one time the stone may have had a cross-head fixed to it, possibly by early missionaries seeking to Christianise an existing sacred, though pagan, object. The monolith is a single block of rough-hewn grit, whose nearest possible source is at least ten miles away near Scarborough. It was probably erected, for ritualistic or religious purposes, in Bronze Age times. Claiming to be the largest standing stone in Britain, it measures 25¾ feet above the ground, and Sir William Strickland, experimenting in the late eighteenth century, estimated it would have an almost similar length in the ground. At ground level it measures an average of five and a half feet by two and a half feet.

No church at Rudston was recorded in the Domesday survey, but one was built soon after the Conquest by William Peveril, lord of the manor. Of this building, part of the tower survives as well as the drum-like font. The north and south aisles were added to the nave around the middle of the thirteenth century, with the chancel being rebuilt in the fourteenth century. Jane Constable left £1, in 1540, to 'repair the body of the church'. The chancel was in a poor state in 1676, and the whole building had badly deteriorated by 1700. In 1748 a gallery was built, probably to house the parish orchestra, which was known to exist for many years. A major repair followed in 1829, and G. Fowler Jones gave it the full Victorian restoration treatment in 1861, the very ornate reredos of Ancaster stone, with panels of Minton tiles, being added in 1869.

Some monuments are worth noting. Two brasses on the wall of the tower vestry commemorate Sir William Constable, of Caythorpe, 1527, and his wife Jane, 1540, although this date was never filled in. Sir Alexander Bosville MacDonald of the Isles was organist of this church for 46 years, and part of a window in the chancel depicts Sir Alexander at the organ. In 1955 a modern memorial window was inserted in the south aisle; and the organ he gave to the church last century has been rebuilt as a further memorial to his services.

Near the font a modern tablet on the wall commemorates Winifred Holtby, 1898–1935, and bears these words: 'Born at Rudston House in this village, educated at Queen Margaret's School, Scarborough, and Somerville College, Oxford, she won a high place amongst the writers of her day. Her work was notable for understanding, insight, and sincerity. Her charm as a woman came from gentle grace of manner, high courage and purpose, practical sympathy for others, and an endearing selflessness. Some of the many who called her friend or who knew her through her writings, have set here this tribute to her memory. Beatti Immaculati'. This was erected by the Winifred Holtby Society. She is buried in a simple grave at the western edge of the churchyard, with the village of her birth and youth across a quiet meadow. A marbled open book on the grave bears the words:

'God give me work till my life shall end
And life till my work is done.'

Sir Alexander MacDonald of the Isles lies close by in his family grave.

Winifred Holtby was born at Rudston House, a large detached farmhouse on the western edge of the village. Her father farmed over 900 acres of Wold country – a substantial sized holding for those days. Village life was still quite feudal, and Winifred grew up in an atmosphere in which duty and service to others were instinctive priorities. Mr. Holtby retired early in Winifred's life, to live at Cottingham, and her mother filled her days by sitting as first woman alderman on the East Riding County Council. In the Prefatory Letter with which she introduces her last and greatest novel, *South Riding*, Winifred admits that 'it was through listening to your descriptions of your work that the drama of English local government first captured my imagination . . . When I came to consider local government, I began to see how it was in essence the first line of defence thrown up by the community against our common enemies – poverty, sickness, ignorance, isolation, mental

17. Beverley Minster from the south. Two centuries of building are in evidence, the east end to the transept c. 1230–60; nave and aisle c. 1300–60; west towers 1390–1430.

derangement, and social maladjustment'. She ends her letter by recording 'one perfect thing: the proud delight which it has meant to me to be the daughter of Alice Holtby'.

Although Rudston lies just north of its boundary, it is the landscape of Holderness which *South Riding* portrays, and against which its characters play out their parts. The southern part of Holderness in particular is used, with Hornsea and Withernsea becoming the fictitious 'Kiplington', and Hull the 'Kingsport' of the novel. Winifred Holtby's five earlier novels have never achieved the fame of her last one, and she did not live to enjoy her eventual success for *South Riding* was published the year after her death.

The best view of Rudston, and the Wolds beyond, is from the hedgerow behind Winifred Holtby's grave. Cloud shadows dapple the ripening corn in summer, and the warm tones of roofs and buildings complete a peaceful requiem. Opposite the church and surrounded by its very neat garden, is the Rudston National School, of 1858. At Thorpe Hall, between Boynton and Rudston, formerly the home of the Bosvilles, the Gypsey Race flows through the grounds where two lakes have been made. The house itself, which stands back from the road, is early eighteenth-century, and has an early nineteenth-century octagonal dairy, now rather neglected on the outside.

The Romano-British farmhouse at Rudston was first discovered as long ago as 1838–9, when walls, tiles, plaster, and some mosaic floor fragments were found. It was almost a century later, however, that many more important discoveries were unearthed by a local farmer in the same field as before, to the south of the Rudston–Kilham road. When eventually uncovered, this 1933 find revealed an almost complete mosaic floor, now known as the Venus Pavement, the goddess of love being shown at her toilet in the central roundel. In the same year, a second mosaic floor was found, known as the Geometric Pavement. A third one was also discovered in the cold room of the bath-house. This mosaic has a water-lily border surrounding a fish tank, and is naturally called the Aquatic Pavement. All three mosaics, together with the excavations at the Roman villa, were open to the public in the later 1930s.

18. Watton Priory: north-west turret and five-sided window of the 15th-century Prior's Hall, now a private house.

In 1959, the late Professor Sir Ian Richmond pointed out that the Roman pavements at Rudston were deteriorating badly. The Ancient Monuments Department of the Ministry of Works, although scheduling the remains, had neither accepted guardianship of them nor had spent anything on them, and advised the transfer of the pavements to the nearest museum, and Hull Museums agreed to do this. Since 1963 they have been on display in the Archaeology section of the Transport Museum housed in the former Corn Exchange building in the old High Street, Hull.

Excavations were continued in 1971, this time on the north side of the Rudston–Kilham road, resulting in the rather surprising discovery that the main living quarters of the house were over there, some 70 or 80 yards from the position of the earlier finds. Two rooms have been investigated, each producing mosaic floors. One is called the Second Geometric Pavement, and the other the Charioteer mosaic, because of the remarkable figure in its central four foot roundel. This shows the frontal view of a Roman circus chariot drawn by four horses, with the standing figure of the charioteer holding in one hand a palm, in the other a wreath, both victory symbols. In the whole mosaic, four main colours are used, with five secondary ones, combining to give richness and subtlety of rare quality, and embracing the use of about 100,000 small stone cubes.

After a very complicated but highly successful lifting operation, both mosaics were transferred to the Hull Museum, where they are now excellently displayed, together with their predecessors from Rudston, and parts of the very large Brantingham pavement.

Kilham Lane continues as a good road south-westwards to Kilham village, whose size and street pattern indicate an earlier importance. Strategically situated between the Wolds and the plain of Holderness, Kilham was a meeting-place for the lowland buyers and the Wold farmers, and in the seventeenth century an important sheep fair was held there every All Saints Day, when large numbers of the small, hardy Wold sheep would change hands. In the middle of the eighteenth century

Kilham, with over 100 families, could be regarded as a small market town. But its market cross has been moved from Kilham to Lowthorpe, three miles away to the south of the Bridlington–Driffield road. Some mystery exists about this move, and one explanation is that the Black Death affected the East Riding, with Kilham being particularly hard-hit. As a result, it was decided to hold the market at Lowthorpe, so the market cross went as well. When the market eventually returned to Kilham the cross stayed at its new site.

Kilham church stands high on a mound near the centre of the village and to its east, almost sunk into the grass bank, is the old bull-ring fixed to a big square block of stone. The Norman doorway of the church has five full orders of carving, and there is a lot of further zig-zag work built into the tower which has a fine array of corbels. The barn-like nave is late Norman, the chancel late thirteenth century.

Lowthorpe church stands remote from its village in a lonely situation, backed by new plantations of fir and spruce. Indeed, it seems almost surrounded by woods, and is reached along a drive between spruce trees. Sir John de Heslerton made this a collegiate church in 1333 for a rector and six priests and the chancel, now ruined, was originally the college chapel. Just inside the south door is a remarkable monument carved on a gravestone at least a foot thick. It represents a man and woman lying beneath a coverlet which itself is covered by a tree growing downwards from the shoulders, with branches extending sideways from the central trunk, each branch ending with a face. The faces are thought to be those of the 13 children of the fourteenth-century Sir Thomas Heslerton, whose memorial this is supposed to be. Another monument is in the nave, a 26 inch brass portrait of a knight in fifteenth-century armour. The Kilham Cross is probably that outside the east end of the chancel. Lowthorpe village has some pleasant, widely scattered houses, the Lodge being Tudor-style, and below the village, by Kelk Beck, an eighteenth-century mill, now a farm.

Harpham is a mile away, on the opposite side of Kelk Beck. The estate here belonged to the St Quintins from Edward II's days until last century, but of their house there is no trace above ground. Their family memorials in the St Quintin Chapel of the church are famous, and include the finest brass in the East Riding which commemorates Sir Thomas de St Quintin and his wife, 1418, with a figure four foot long beneath a double canopy. There is a slightly smaller brass to Thomas de St Quintin, 1445. When Temple Moore restored the church prior to 1914, the eighteenth-century furnishings, box pews, pulpit, and altar rails of 1726 were allowed to remain.

From the crossroads north of Harpham, it is only a mile to Burton Agnes, where the main road curves through a series of bends and passes by some splendid trees overlooking a large village pond where notices point to Burton Agnes Hall.

The gatehouse is dated 1610, and is broader than it is high. On it a stone coat-of-arms of James I flanked by two allegorical figures contrasts with the mellowed brick. Within the grounds a straight path between lawns and yews of the eighteenth century gives a splendid approach to the south front. Although only eight bays wide, the enormously projecting end bays seem to extend like welcoming arms, giving a first impression of homeliness, which a closer acquaintance merely helps to emphasise.

Burton Agnes has never been bought or sold. From the date of the first Norman manor, 1173, ownership has passed from one family to another, should the male line come to an end, and it has been in the family of Mr Wickham-Boynton, its present owner, for about four centuries. Its first owner was Roger de Stuteville, recorded in a deed of 1175. His eldest daughter married a Roger de Merlay, whose male line ended after three generations, when Burton Agnes passed to Robert de Somerville, of Wichnor in Staffordshire; and subsequently by marriage to the Griffiths. Although they owned Burton Agnes, they remained in the Midlands, until Sir Walter Griffith moved to the old Manor House which he made habitable once more. It was Sir Henry Griffith, born in 1559, who, on his appointment to the Council of the North which was based at York, decided to rebuild Burton Agnes. A plan of the house was discovered among the papers of Robert Smithson, who was responsible for Longleat, Hardwick, and Wollaton, and was, of course, Master Mason to Queen Elizabeth.

Burton Agnes has been very little changed during the centuries, and by placing the front door at the side of one of the smaller projecting bays, the symmetry of the beautiful south front has been retained. About 1730 the levels of the central part of the house were altered to give a low storey between the ground floor and the upper one, accounting for its shallow windows. These, like the others in the centre bays, and all of those of the east front, were sashed at the same time. The Palladian windows at each end of the Long Gallery on the upper floor were also introduced then. The date 1601, with the initials of Sir Henry Griffith and his lady, appears above the entrance, while 1610 is shown in the frieze of one of the bedrooms, so the building had virtually been completed by then.

The Hall has been open to the public since 1949, two years after Mr Wickham-Boynton took it over from his mother, who rather sadly had allowed it to run down. Since then, the number of visitors has risen to about 30,000 a year – nowhere near the top of the 'Stately Homes League Table', but very satisfactory when its rather out-of-the-way situation is considered. For over 25 years, the owner has restored and refurnished it room by room, with the aim of making it both look and feel comfortable. For major restoration work he has had only one major Historic Buildings grant, the rest having come from the increasing prosperity of the horse stud founded by his father, and built by himself into a most successful business. He has sold over £1 million worth of thoroughbreds, and now runs 13 brood mares, with four racehorses in training.

Finest of all the rooms of the house is the magnificent Long Gallery, now restored to its full length of 100 feet – the complete width of the south front. Its reconstruction has meant removing seven other rooms which had been occupied as servants' quarters since 1810. From a surviving fragment of the original stucco ceiling which had collapsed, a Leeds firm has been able to make the beautiful barrel ceiling of today. The internal early Georgian woodwork has come from Kilnwick Hall, Driffield, and other furnishings have been bought in, so that once more there is an elegance which reflects the owner's careful selection of furniture, porcelain, bronzes, and chandeliers.

To the west of the Hall, a plain rectangular building in seventeenth-century brickwork hides the original Manor House of late Norman times. Now in the guardianship of the Department of the Environment, it is open at all reasonable times, and admission is free. You go directly into the dark undercroft where short but massive round piers fling chamfered ribs across the vaulted and groined roof. There is a stone chimney-breast at the back, and from the north-west corner of the undercroft a dark spiral stair leads to the upper room which was probably added in the fifteenth century by Sir Walter Griffith, and of which the original timber roof survives.

There is at least one more surprise at Burton Agnes Hall. In a corner behind the old Manor House is a donkey-wheel. Originally used for raising water from the adjacent well, it consists of a large wheel with wooden 'flooring' wide enough to be trodden by a donkey walking inside it, causing it to turn, and thus raising or lowering a rope wound round its axle. The wheel is protected by a tiled roof supported by a simple post, strut and beam arrangement.

The parish church of St Martin is north-west of the Hall, reached by a road leading to its dark yew walk approach. Most of the building is Norman, the piers of the north arcade being similar to those of the old Manor House. The battlemented clerestory and the tower are Perpendicular, the north side of the chancel is of eighteenth-century brick, but the rest is early Victorian. It is scarcely surprising that there should be such a rich collection of memorials, most of them at the east end of the north aisle. On the north wall of the Boynton Chapel Sir Henry Griffith, 1645, and his two ladies are commemorated, not by effigies, but by the macabre feature of three black coffins. Most of the inscriptions refer to the many noble families connected with the Griffiths and the Boyntons, the tomb chests and the stained-glass windows carrying emblems of their various shields. By cool contrast, in the south aisle there is a beautiful memorial, not to a member of these families, but to a vicar of Burton Agnes, Thomas Dade, 1759 – a tablet, urn, and obelisk of very fine detail by an unknown craftsman. Outside, the churchyard has been cleared of its headstones – over 60 of them – which have been re-erected round its border.

Two miles east of Driffield, and lying just south of the main road, Nafferton is another village like Kilham, of greater importance once than it is now. The Naffers are a series of clear springs welling from the chalk in and around the village, to amalgamate and form Nafferton Beck. The road running southwards through the village turns a number of corners, so that at any one time only part of the village is seen. Such an arrangement, unplanned, informal, representing a natural organic growth, yields a variety of views and street names – High Street, Middle Street, North Street, Westgate, Priestgate, Coppergate. Many houses have date-stones of the eighteenth century, and their dark-coloured brickwork has mellowed attractively.

When the Hull–Bridlington branch of the York and North Midland Railway was opened in 1846, it passed through Nafferton, where the station and its adjoining house were designed by G. T. Andrews in a simpler style than those he built at Market Weighton and Pocklington. The house has a portico with four Tuscan pillars supporting a canopy, a style repeated at some other East Riding village stations. Towering above it, on the opposite side of the level-crossing, is Station Mill, built in 1878 as the first rail-side cornmill in the district, and having grindstones installed in it. This was a costly error, for these were already out-of-date, being replaced in other mills by rollers more suited to dealing with the foreign wheat then being imported in large quantities to cater for the demands of an increasing population. Rollers also produced a finer, whiter flour, but it was not until 1890 that they were installed at the Nafferton Mill. The great brick building also housed a small malting which, early this century was converted into a silo granary and warehouse, and now animal feeds are also produced there.

An even more impressive five-storey building, Nafferton Maltings, dominates the village on its eastern side. This dates from 1840, a combined maltings and cornmill, operated by

water-power from Nafferton Beck, subsequently supplemented by steam-power, but in 1900 the corn-milling
ceased, and only the malting was continued. That ended in
1966. Animal feeds are now produced there and the owners
have restored the water wheel. The pair of malt kilns crowns
one end, and a smaller drying-kiln at the other make a starkly
dramatic skyline.

These nineteenth-century industrial buildings are at the
opposite end of the village to the large church, which, standing
on a high bank, looks down on the pantiled roofs of the houses,
its Perpendicular west tower dominating the scene. Like so
many East Riding churches, All Saints, Nafferton presents a
better picture outside than in, although there are box pews, a
Norman font with crude carving, and a huge squint.

By continuing south from Nafferton you soon join the
Driffield–Skipsea road, B.1249, at Wansford, where G. E.
Street designed the church in 1868 for Sir Tatton Sykes,
together with the parsonage and school, which make an attractive group in this flat landscape. Nafferton Beck flows into the
River Hull, and the white-washed, pantiled mill, with willows
growing by the water, makes a Constable-like scene, especially
with afternoon sunshine texturing the walls with glancing
light.

The road back to Driffield follows the Driffield Canal, where
easy access to the banks makes it a favourite place for fishermen. The canal looks in a healthy condition and enthusiasts
would like to see it used once more as a navigable waterway. It
was around 1765 that the corn merchants of Driffield and
Kilham were anxious to have the upper reaches of the River
Hull made navigable for keels to reach Driffield. An Act of 1767
allowed for the construction of the Driffield Navigation, five
miles of waterway from the River Hull near North Frodingham
to Driffield itself, together with a short stretch of the Frodingham Beck. Like other East Riding waterways the Driffield
Navigation provided water transport for grain and other
agricultural produce down to the industrial towns of the
Humber, the keels returning with coal, fertilisers, building
materials, and groceries. The commissioners who administered

the Canal were concerned for the agricultural interest of the area which it served, and made concessions on the tolls for some goods carried. They also encouraged the building of warehouses and granaries at the head of the canal at Driffield, of which some late eighteenth-century ones still exist to form a splendid group of industrial buildings.

When the railway was brought to Driffield, canal tolls were reduced in order to compete. This had the effect of keeping the railway rates down, and canal trade was inevitably lost to its quicker service. But the commissioners never neglected their waterway. Indeed, a steam dredger was bought in 1898, with the hope of deepening the navigation so that steam-propelled barges could use it. However, most of its grain trade was gone by 1900, although sailing keels, and a few powered ones, continued to use the canal until about 1942, and water-borne trade to Driffield ended in the 1950s. Although four locks have deteriorated, the actual channel is kept in good condition because, since 1960, it has helped to provide millions of gallons of drinking water daily for Hull.

Now, the canal-head wharves and warehouses form the most attractive part of Great Driffield. The canal's feeder-stream flows through a culvert beneath the road at the south end of the town, with the canal basin dominated by the two great grain warehouses of E. B. Bradshaw and Sons. One of these, on the west bank of the canal, has just been converted, most tastefully and imaginatively, into flats – an admirable use for a fine industrial structure no longer able to fulfil the needs for which it was built. Beyond it is ample car-parking space near a well-kept grassy area along the canal bank, where a large wharfside crane evokes memories of a much greater activity than the present swans and ornamental fish would be able to tolerate. The scene is a visual asset, but it would be much better if the Navigation could be restored as an amenity waterway over its entire length, and not just the short stretch below Brigham which is used by the local sailing club.

Great Driffield regards itself, with some justification, as 'the capital of the Wolds'. Yet 200 years ago it was a village with a population of just 800, one tenth of what it is today. However, three events occurred in 1772 which started the growth of Driffield's fortunes and importance. Although the Driffield Navigation was opened in May 1770, troubles with lock gates had meant that it was not an effective waterway for trade to the town until June 1772. It is interesting to speculate what would have happened if the initial money for the canal had not been used up, for it was originally intended to take it as far as Kilham, a much more important wool centre and market town. But Kilham's loss was Driffield's gain: a market town became a quiet village; a village prospered into a thriving market town and agricultural centre.

Also in 1772, John Wesley preached in the Market Place, giving encouragement to the small groups of local methodists who up till then were meeting in one another's homes. As a result, methodism rapidly grew to become a powerful local force, at exactly the same time as local trade increased. The Market Place then presented a different picture from today, for there were two-storied houses, and some thatched cottages. Opposite The Bell Hotel was a general shop which, in 1772, became Driffield's first Post Office. Before then, mail had come fortnightly from Kilham by an old woman with her donkey (weather permitting), postage being paid by the recipient. The starting of this new Post Office was the third event of 1772 which turned the history of Driffield.

The town had for some centuries provided one of the outlets for the produce of farmers on the thinly populated Wolds to the north and west so that Driffield was a focus for a fairly self-sufficient community. With the improvement in communications brought about first by the Driffield Navigation, and then, in 1846, by the bringing of the railway from Hull to Bridlington, followed a few years later by the opening of a line to Malton, Driffield developed as the centre for a number of industries associated with farming. Corn-milling, malting barley, and brewing of beer, the manufacture and repair of agricultural implements, and the supply of animal feeds, fertilisers, and seeds, all these were soon well established in the town. Driffield was the grain-milling centre for much of the East Riding by the middle of last century, and to house the growing population many new streets were built eastwards from the original three streets of the town, Middle Street, containing the Market Place, Westgate to the west of the church, and Eastgate on the other side of the Beck.

There are now the usual supermarkets, the chromium, plastic, plate-glass frontages of the shops in Middle Street and the Market Place. But some older façades persist at first- and second-floor level, while around the Market Place the banks and the inns contrast with a few Georgian and some good Victorian shop fronts. Further to the north, Middle Street becomes narrower before suddenly presenting you with a view of the massive, dark stone dignity of the Parish Church. To appreciate this best you need to be able to stand back, either down the broad street to the east, or in the narrower Church Street to the west, and then look up at the great west tower, at 110 feet one of the highest in Yorkshire, fifteenth-century, buttressed, with pinnacles and battlements. Inside the church is mainly early thirteenth-century, with fragments from the earlier Norman structure re-used. By way of contrast, the Weslyan Chapel, tucked away in a little lane between the Market Place and the church, is what Pevsner calls 'a swaggering piece' of 1880 with an enormous Ionic front.

South of the station the huge maltings ceased to operate as such in 1960, but has since been used as a grain store. Another large factory, built in 1862 for the manufacture of linseed cake, closed in 1940, was taken over by a sugar firm during the Second World War, and is now a club's premises. Thus the old big buildings manage to survive, but the railway line to Malton and York has gone, and only the line to Hull and Bridlington remains. Driffield prospered for almost two centuries because of its importance in a communications system involving canal and railway. Now it stands where main roads from York, Selby and Hull meet to become the one important road from inland Yorkshire to Bridlington. On summer Saturdays the town becomes the familar bottle-neck, and the pleasure of walking in its old streets is gone.

CHAPTER SEVEN

Sledmere and the Northern Wolds

The York road to the west, the A.166, leads past Little Driffield towards the open landscape of the Wolds. Villages are some miles apart, and the prosperous-looking farms, within the rectangular protection of their shelter-belts, stand well back, surrounded by their eighteenth-century-enclosed fields. Garton-on-the-Wold, three miles from Driffield, is a street village with a Street church, originally established by Kirkham Priory in 1132, and largely restored for the first Sir Tatton Sykes by Pearson in 1856–7. The second Sir Tatton brought in Street in 1865, and he was responsible for the imitation thirteenth-century fresco which meets with Pevsner's unguarded approval.

Beyond Garton the road forks, the A.166 keeping due west for Wetwang and Fridaythorpe to which we shall return. The more important fork for us is that leading north-west to Sledmere, for it is time we looked at this most famous area of Wold country, the rich expansive acres of the Sykes estates.

Until the eighteenth century the Wolds here were largely a bare, uncultivated landscape. Since then, successive generations of the Sykes family have enclosed it, tended it, and have made it prosper to become one of the best agricultural areas in Britain. Their memorial lies all around you as you travel the four miles from Garton to Sledmere. The most spectacular of the Sykes monuments, a Wolds landmark for miles around, a slender tower, 120 feet high of grey and brown stone, erected by the tenantry in 1865, commemorates the fourth baronet, Sir

102

Tatton Sykes, who died two years earlier. Vaguely Gothic, with panels in relief at the base of its four-sided tower showing Sir Tatton surveying his estates, it tapers towards the top. An internal stairway leads to a high room with oriels; above this is a pinnacle crowned by a very elaborate cross, the whole being designed by J. Gibbs of Oxford.

The fortunes of the Sykes family started, appropriately, in wool, with William Sykes (born 1500) at Leeds. His grandson Richard, bought the Manor of Leeds from the Crown in the seventeenth century; his fortunes prospered so that he could hand over huge estates to his four sons, and provide four daughters each with a £10,000 dowry. A later Richard Sykes inherited the Tudor house at Sledmere in 1748. His father had married Mary Kirkby, a descendant of Sir Robert Kirkby of Cottingham and heiress of the Sledmere estates. Richard Sykes was born in 1706, and was High Sheriff of Yorkshire in 1752, by when plans had been prepared to change the house and its parklands.

He demolished the original manor-house, replacing it with a Queen Anne-style house in brick, with stone facings, making a seven-bay-square block, none of which is now visible from the outside. When Richard died in 1761 he was succeeded by his brother, Mark, who was vicar of Roos (Richard being the patron of the living). In 1783, the Reverend Mark Sykes became the only clergyman to be made a baronet – an honour which arose largely at the request of his son, Christopher, who had actually been offered it by William Pitt in recognition of his pioneering agricultural work on the estates which he had taken over from his father in 1776.

Sir Mark Sykes died in 1783, and it was Sir Christopher, possibly guided by the architect Wyatt, who gave Sledmere House its present form. Two wings were added to the north and south, and the whole structure was faced in Nottinghamshire stone. The southern wing became the entrance front with hall and staircase running down at right angles to it, and principal rooms on either side. Taking up the whole of the first floor was the great library, the spaciously elegant heart of the Georgian house. Sir Christopher had laid the foundations of the fine collection of rare books as a result of his 1770 Grand Tour, his son, Sir Mark Masterman Sykes, adding greatly to it between 1801 and 1823.

By 1787 the house was completed, and Joseph Rose, who had worked with the Adam brothers, was commissioned to decorate it. A disastrous fire in 1911 destroyed a great deal of the interior, although all the movable contents were saved, including Rose's original drawings for the plasterwork. From these the York architect, W. H. Brierly, was able to recreate Rose's decorative work, as well as other restoration in the original form, apart from the entrance hall which he re-designed. Most of the furnishings and paintings in the various rooms to which the public are admitted are eighteenth-century, with some from the sixteenth and seventeenth centuries, and the whole interior of the house reflects the cultured tastes of the successive members of this family of country squires.

After the fire, a further 40 rooms were added, mainly in brick, but in 1945 it was decided to demolish them as being unnecessary for the family requirements of post-war times. The materials went into the construction of twelve modern estate cottages in the village, and the site they formerly covered is now an Italian garden around a fountain.

Before Sir Christopher's additions to the house he had engaged Capability Brown to lay out a 2,000-acre park. The plan necessitated the demolition of every house in Sledmere village which was situated by the old York road. By 1787 a new village was built around the northern edge of the park, with the York road passing through on the course it now follows, so within a few years huge changes had taken place in this heart of the Wolds countryside.

Christopher Sykes had married Elizabeth Tatton, joint heiress of the Egerton estates, and it was some of her huge fortune which encouraged him to start his pioneering work in agriculture. With the enclosing of vast sheep-walks on the Wolds around Sledmere he was able to start large-scale ploughing and cultivation, in which he experimented with grass leys and the growing of barley; over 54,000 larch trees were planted as copses and shelter-belts; many new farms, barns, and stables were erected, and miles of new roads were constructed. It was characteristic of him to insist that these had wide grass verges in order that poor people could graze their stock. By the time of his death in 1801 he owned 34,000 acres of splendid land, with his house in its park forming a wooded island near the centre.

In Sledmere village there is a domed memorial by the roadside opposite the main entrance to the house. Its inscription reads: 'This edifice was erected by Sir Tatton Sykes, baronet, to the memory of his Father, Sir Christopher Sykes, baronet, who, by assiduity and perservance in building and planting and inclosing on the Yorkshire Wolds in the short space of 30 years set such an example to other owners of land as he has caused what was once a blank and barren tract of country to become now one of the most productive and best cultivated districts in the County of York. A.D.1840'.

The third baronet, Sir Mark Masterman Sykes, established in 1801 the Sledmere Stud. After his death in 1823 his brother, Sir Tatton Sykes continued to increase it until it exceeded 300 head and was the largest in England. This fourth baronet became a legendary figure throughout Yorkshire, an ideal squire, and a man of immense energy and determination. One morning he rode the 63 miles from Sledmere to Pontefract to take part in a race during the afternoon. He then went to Doncaster, stayed the night, continuing to Lincoln for a four-mile race that afternoon. On two occasions he rode to Aberdeen to take part in Scotland's greatest race, the Welter Stakes. Immediately afterwards he rode back to Doncaster each time in order to see his own horses competing in the St Leger. His frequent journeys to London took him four days from Sledmere, while nearer home he often rode about his estates as a drover for his own sheep – and he dressed the part!

After his death in 1861, his son, the second Sir Tatton, cleared out the stables, except for one original mare. Others from new strains helped to set up another stud which has produced innumerable top-class horses. The present baronet Sir Richard Sykes, is particularly interested in the breeding of bloodstock. It was the second Sir Tatton Sykes who was a social pioneer, with special interest in education and the church. He built five new schools, enlarged two others, and paid for their maintenance over a number of years. There are more than 20 churches throughout the East Riding which he built or restored, 12 on the Sledmere estates. His father had already employed Pearson to restore Kirkburn and Garton-on-the-Wolds, but the second Sir Tatton went to Street for his work, followed by Hodgson Fowler and Temple Moore, who was responsible for the church at Sledmere itself. A rather gloomy building, south-west of the house, and just off the main road through the village, it retains some older work in the lower part of the west tower, while a number of Norman corbels are built into the wall of a room above the organ. Nave and chancel are wagon-roofed, the porch elaborately vaulted, and there are naturally many family monuments.

Temple Moore also designed the ornamental structure on the green opposite the church gate, a copy of the Eleanor Cross at Northampton with brass plaques added to it in 1919 to convert it into a war memorial. A few yards along the road is the war memorial of 1919 to Sir Mark Sykes' 'Company of Wagoners'. In 1912, about 1,200 farm men of the Yorkshire Wolds volunteered for Sir Mark's 'Wagoners' Reserve', ready to be called up, if needed, for transport work involving horses. They were paid a retaining fee of a £1 a year, and soon after the Great War started they were in France. Near the end of the war, Sir Mark Sykes prepared plans for a 'Wolds Wagoners' Memorial, which would portray the men and their work. An Italian sculptor, Carlo Magnani, helped by the estate stonemason, translated Sir Mark's drawings into stone. A cylindrical centrepiece with four columns and a spire, shows a series of war-stories carved in relief, and round the circumference is a circular stone tapestry of homely history which Sir Mark did not live to see completed.

Sir Mark Sykes, the sixth baronet, spread his brilliance over a much wider area. When he was a young man he travelled extensively through the Middle East, where the knowledge and connections he gained were especially useful during the Great War. The statesman-like qualities of his fine intellect

Top: left (19)   old corn mill at Stamford Bridge on the River Derwent, now a restaurant; *right* (20)   Knedlington Old Hall, an early 17th-century brick house near Howden. *Bottom* (21)   Howsham Hall: the south front of 1619, showing Jacobean symmetry and fenestration.

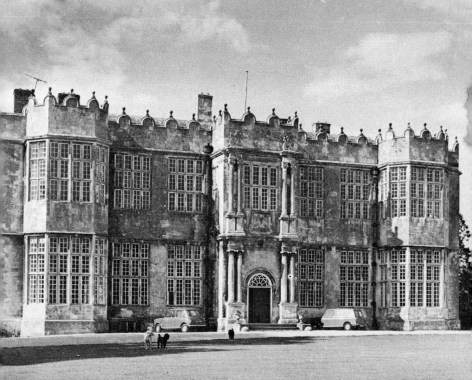

were added to his disciplined sense of duty as a soldier, and the British Government sent him on delicate negotiations to Egypt, Arabia, and Syria, resulting in the Sykes-Picot Agreement of 1916. He also helped to start the Arab Bureau, which led to T. E. Lawrence going out to take charge of the Arab revolt. Sir Mark died when only 39 at the 1919 Versailles Peace Conference. The Turkish Room at Sledmere is largely his memorial, its walls covered with Damascus tiles. Various papers associated with Sir Mark's Middle East diplomacy are also displayed.

Sir Richard Sykes is the seventh baronet and a former High Sheriff of Yorkshire. He opened Sledmere House to the public in 1965. Apprehensive at first, he has found that the many thousands of people who annually visit it have had remarkably little effect on his family's private life. The visitors show a meticulous respect for everything, not least for the fact that this lovely place has been the home of a happy family through many turbulent generations of English history. Still at the centre of an estate which is now about 12,000 acres, Sledmere will retain its family, for Sir Richard has four sons – the eldest named Tatton – and two daughters.

A good road, the B.1251, leads south-west from Sledmere village along the western edge of the park, curving down to a roundabout, where it is crossed by the B.1249. Two miles down this takes us to Wetwang, a typical Wolds village extending for half a mile along a broad street flanked by eighteenth- and nineteenth-century houses. Ponds at each end are of ancient origin and the lychgate to the churchyard contains fragments of coffin lids. The church itself retains some Norman work, and was restored for Sir Tatton Sykes by Fowler in 1901–2.

Westwards along the A.166, Fridaythorpe stands more than 500 feet up, a village which seems to have lost some of its former Wolds character. The ponds remain, but the best corner of the village lies north, away from the main road. A simple church hides behind a farm and some beech trees, retaining some Norman work, including what Pevsner describes as a 'barbaric south door . . . decorated . . . with any old thing going'. Fowler carried out a restoration in 1902 for Sir Tatton

22. Looking north across the Wolds near Huggate at harvest-time.

Sykes and included in it the rather nice sundial. Two miles to the north-east, Fimber has another Sykes church, a Street restoration of 1871, with an attractive stone lychgate. There is a particularly good brass chancel screen, and the bust of Sir Tatton looks approvingly from a window-sill.

The Ordnance Survey Map names some of the former open fields on the Wolds. Near Fimber is South Field, with Fridaythorpe Field to its west and Towthorpe Field to the north. Between the various Wolds, dry, grassy valleys wind their ways, some of them now with quiet lanes offering fascinating routes either for walking or motoring. From Fimber and Fridaythorpe such lanes can be followed westwards to Thixendale; that from Fimber is parallel to the old Burdale— Wharram railway in a steep-sided valley locally called Fimber Bottom. Like the other narrow valleys, this is mainly uncultivated grassland with gorse bushes, a few hawthorns and a fringe of trees along the crest where the thin soil has been ploughed and the Wold tops sown with wheat and barley.

Thixendale is one of the most isolated of all the villages in these northern Wolds, yet six minor roads lead to it, and it has the remarkable distinction of being centred on a network of 16 dry valleys. Malton is its nearest town, ten miles away, and there is no bus service. When winter snows descend it is not unknown for it to be isolated for weeks at a time. Only a small village along a short stretch of the valley bottom where a clear chalk stream flows, it used to have its own water supply collected from springs at the bottom of the hillside, fed into a concrete tank, which then supplied eight taps in the village street, the surplus continuing as a stream through the village. The church of 1870 is by Street for Sir Tatton Sykes, very much in 1300 style. He also designed the lychgate, the vicarage, and the school which make a pleasant group on the south side of the road.

Thixendale's greatest attraction is its situation, and a good view of this is obtained from the brow of the hill to the east of the village, on the road to Fimber. Pantiled roofs and house groupings contrast with the green contours of the steep valley and the Wolds beyond. Any of the three roads running generally west from Thixendale eventually lead up to the higher Wolds and the 700 foot contour. If you take the Fridaythorpe road from the east of the village and keep right along that signposted to Painsthorpe, you can again savour the delights of a quiet valley. In half a mile you can turn left off this road and walk a section of the long-distance path, the Wolds Way, merely to sample what is becoming a popular stretch of walking country in the heart of the Wolds. If you prefer to keep to the road you will climb up on to Thixendale Wold, and near Painsthorpe will reach the Roman road which ran for 25 miles between Malton and South Newbald.

Villages are more numerous along the spring-line foot of the Wolds, with narrow, steep and winding lanes sweeping down to them. Kirby Underdale is the most southerly of these villages, a mile below the Roman road, beyond the hamlet of Painsthorpe. There are wide views northwards along the Wold escarpment, but Kirby Underdale itself hides secretively in a deep hollow, with a church, unusually in the Wold country, set lower down the hillside than the village it serves. Indeed, from the east end of the village you descend a long flight of steps to it, starting almost level with the top of the west tower, where herringbone masonry gives a fair clue to its late eleventh-century origins. There is a lovely little Norman west door, and Street's restoration of 1871 has managed to retain much of the thirteenth- and fourteenth-century work. Nearby, the rectory possesses the seventeenth-century pinnacles which were originally on the church-tower, and the short wide street of the village has some excellent brick houses mainly of early last century, Victorian school buildings closing the view at the west end of the street.

A winding lane leads northwards from Kirby Underdale, gradually climbing back to the Roman road and passing rich plantations on the western slopes. Northwards then, by Hanging Grimston, to reach the 750 foot mark on either Acklam Wold or Leavening Brow, both major viewpoints across the coloured fields of the vale. Acklam Wold yielded an impressive Bronze Age cemetery, with later British entrenchments, in which gold necklaces, amber beads, and jet buttons have been found. Signs of strip lynchets suggest this was marginal land a thousand years ago; now sheep graze on the steep grassy slopes, although some of them have been ploughed up. Acklam village has more stone than brick, which makes a change, and the tightly clustered houses of Leavening present an attractive group, particularly when seen from the Acklam road. Neither village has any claim to fame.

We have come a rather long way round to Leavening. A quicker route from Thixendale, by way of the road up Waterdale, would have brought us here in half the time. From this road, east of Leavening, we can now cut across the edge of Birdsall Brow, and drop down to the splendid parklands of Birdsall House, home of Lord Middleton. You can see part of the house from the road, sufficient to identify its eighteenth-century centre portion, with the two wings added early last century. Originally it was of two storeys, but Salvin added a third around 1875. Close to the house is the ruined church, opposite the stable block. Probably abandoned at the same time as the wings were added to the house, it still retains its Norman chancel arch, and above the tower arch is the date 1601. Its replacement half a mile north on the edge of the park is of 1823, with Fowler adding the chancel in 1880.

North Grimston is less than three miles away to the east, the road passing sites of two Roman villas before joining the B.1248 in the village, just before the church. The Wolds are no great height around here, and being well wooded, present a much less austere landscape. Trees of splendid maturity grow in and near the village, where little bridges cross the stream to the cottages along the street. Six old lime trees mark the path down to the church, a long, low building with a Norman chancel and a thirteenth-century tower. Inside, the walls and arches lean, particularly the chancel arch, much wider at the top than the bottom and with good zig-zag carving. That apart, it is the massive Norman font that catches the eye, three feet in diameter, lopsided, with quaint carving round its drum-like exterior, mostly showing the Last Supper.

Mention has already been made of some deserted villages. Three miles from North Grimston is one of the most famous of them all, Wharram Percy. The B.1248 leads south-east on to the Wolds to Wharram-le-Street, whose church contains Saxon and Norman work. Beyond, a lane leads to Burdale, and just past Bella Farm, a green sign points the way to the deserted medieval village of Wharram Percy, and you will have to walk for half a mile. There is space for a few cars at the beginning of the path, and if you are there during July, it is most likely that you will see some tents on the brow of a field across the valley to the west. They will be the temporary home of the 30 or so volunteers who have come to participate in the excavation of Wharram Percy.

Every summer since 1950 there has been a short season of excavation here, making it the longest continuing excavation in Britain which is organised entirely with unpaid volunteers.

Professor M. W. Beresford, one of the leading experts in the field of medieval villages, described Wharram Percy as 'the most promising of all village sites excavated in England'. That was in 1954, when he had already spent six seasons there. By now, an enormous amount has been discovered, although on the ground the casual observer might not see very much now. The excavations of previous years have been filled in to avoid danger to cattle, and the hillside to the north-west of the current excavations is once more pasture, as it had been before its secrets were revealed.

In its way, Wharram Percy has been as important a milestone in the archaeology of medieval England as were the more spectacular excavations on, say, the Roman Wall, or Maiden Castle in terms of the light they threw on their periods.

The church of St Martin is now the only building of the former village that survives above ground. It served not only Wharram Percy, but the nearby villages of Thixendale, Burdale, Raisthorpe and Towthorpe. The last three are all deserted: only Thixendale remains, and it now has its own church. Wharram Church is no longer used, and it has been handed over by the Church Commissioners to the Department of the Environment for preservation as a ruin. Work on it, and within its churchyard, has been going on since 1962, with the aim of a total excavation to identify all the previous churches.

The early settlement at Wharram Percy was on the hill immediately to the west of the church. Nearby, in the late twelfth century the Percy family built their large manor house, subsequently abandoning it in favour of a site farther up the hill to the north, with an extension of the village several hundred yards north again, where the track to the present church divides as it leaves the wooded valley. The Hilton family acquired the estate in the fifteenth century, re-planned the manorial layout, and probably decreed that the new houses should be gable-end to the street – a right-angled change from their predecessors.

Thus has been revealed the story of just one of over a hundred deserted medieval villages in the East Riding. Like many of them, Wharram Percy was affected by the Black Death around 1350, but this did not completely empty the village. Recent pottery finds show that it was inhabited at least until 1500, when the cloth-making industry was growing rapidly in Yorkshire as elsewhere. More wool being needed, it became more profitable for the landowners to concentrate on sheep-rearing rather than growing corn. This made ploughmen redundant, so the village lost the livelihood of its menfolk, and the 1,500 acres of the parish gradually became an enormous sheep-run. The houses soon collapsed, and grass grew over them. By the end of the eighteenth century the wheel had turned full cycle again, and under the new large landowners, the Middletons, improved farming methods brought Wharram's acres under plough again. Now, most of the lands of the former Wharram village make up the single 1,000-acre farm of Wharram Percy which stands securely among its trees, a mile to the south-west.

The old Malton–Driffield railway line threaded its way along the valley by Wharram Percy, from North Grimston to Burdale. Opened in 1853 the line was quite an engineering triumph, since steep gradients had to be negotiated as well as the mile-long Burdale Tunnel, which took six years to build. It proved its worth, especially in winter, to the farmers of the Wolds, and it also carried away huge quantities of chalk from the quarries at Burdale and Wharram. The last passenger train ran in 1950, but it was another eight years before goods traffic ceased.

Wharram Quarry, last worked in the 1940s, is now a nature reserve leased from the Birdsall Estate Company Limited to the Yorkshire Naturalists' Trust, whose members have free access to it. Unaccompanied non-members require a permit. Its flat floor and steep cliff, with scooped hollows, have created a varied habitat showing a succession of stages in the development of a chalk soil. The old working face is gradually acquiring a vegetative cover, while the hollows in it have provided a home for ash, wild apple and wild gooseberry.

From Wharram-le-Street, we can explore eastwards in the Wold Valley, aiming first for Duggleby, a hamlet on the Sledmere road. In one respect it merits attention, for 200 yards south-east of Duggleby Church, just off the main road, is one of the largest round barrows ever found in Britain. With a mound 120 feet in diameter and 20 feet high, excavation revealed a pit nine feet deep into the chalk, with a 50-foot diameter pile of rubble containing at least 50 cremation remains, above the bodies of adults and children in the deeper pit. Accompanying the burials were flint arrowheads, blades made from boars' teeth, beavers' teeth, and bone skewer pins.

The Wold Valley is an unusual and impressive feature of these northern Wolds, a shallow but broadening trough carrying a tiny chalk stream which, in southern counties, would be called a bourne. It rises between Wharram-le-Street and Duggleby, flows northwards for a mile, then eastwards to the coast at Bridlington for a distance of 22 miles, normally on the surface to Wold Newton, then underground to Rudston. Long before then it has become known as the Gypsey Race; even longer before it was the course of the River Ure, from Wensleydale.

A minor road accompanies the stream down the Wold Valley, linking the villages which have sited themselves to take advantage of its clear water supply. Their layout differs slightly from that of the villages on the open Wolds, which had two or three large open fields divided into strips, and covered anything from 100 to many thousands acres. These open fields started from very close to the garths of the houses themselves.

In the Wold Valley, however, the arable fields were usually on the Wold slopes close to the village, with the open fields beyond them, higher up on the Wold on both sides of the valley.

Kirby Grindalyth is the first and smallest of the villages; a few farms and cottages, a small manor-house, and a church restored for Sir Tatton Sykes by Street, 1878, who retained the Norman west tower, and medieval belfry, and re-used the masonry in the chancel. At West Lutton, two miles down the valley, the same partnership was again at work, this time producing the only wooden belfry in any of Sykes' churches. A weathercock tops the shingled spire surveying the cluster of farms and cottages grouped close round the pond.

Also from 1874–5 is Street's restoration of the church at Helperthorpe, with Temple Moore adding a north aisle in 1893. This time he gave the west tower a low broach spire, designed the parsonage, and probably the cross in the churchyard.

The Wold Valley stream is a flirtatious thing, lacking the virtue of constancy. By Weaverthorpe, however, it has become more mature as befits one of the larger villages in the valley, where the houses and farms sit snugly into the friendly landscape. Its church – yet another Street restoration for Sir Tatton, 1872 – stands austere and proud on a windy hill north of the village, with a slim early Norman tower, Northumbrian in simplicity and having a rounded stair-turret. There is good Norman work inside, tower arch and nave, chancel arch and chancel, and drum-like font. The open-wagon type roof has 26 ribs in the nave and 15 in the chancel, all richly coloured. Above the lintel of the doorway is a tympanum bearing a Saxon sundial whose inscription states that Herbert of Winchester built the church about 1110 in honour of St Andrew.

Three miles east of Weaverthorpe the road along the Wold Valley crosses a bigger road near Foxholes and continues to Wold Newton, where rather more of the small houses in the village than usual are built of chalk quarried locally. The big pond by the crossroads was rather lacking in water when I was there, making it look untidy. Like other villages in the remoter part of the Wolds, this one has very little new building, so although there is no outstanding architecture what there is presents a quietly attractive picture. A church hidden away behind some trees retains much Norman work, including a good south door, a very small font, and a massive chancel arch.

The village has one rare claim to fame, an event commemorated by a brick obelisk placed between two trees in a field about three quarters of a mile to the south-west, and not apparently accessible by public footpath. The inscription is now almost illegible, but it once stated:

Here
On this spot, December 13, 1795
Fell from the atmosphere
An extraordinary stone,
In breadth twenty–eight inches
In length thirty-six inches
And
Whose weight was fifty-six pounds.
This column
In memory of it
Was erected by
Edward Topham
1799

The meteorite fell at 3 p.m. on a misty winter afternoon, and although there was thunder in the distance, the sound of explosion caused by the meteorite's landing 'alarmed the surrounding country and created so distinctly the sensation that something very singular had happened'. A local magistrate, Edward Topham, lived nearby, and both the flight and the landing of the meteorite were witnessed by his shepherd, who was only 150 yards away from where it landed, and by a farmhand called John Shipley who was hit by some soil scattered by the meteorite's crashing into the earth, making a hole a yard in diameter and 19 inches deep.

Mr Topham wrote down these and other accounts of the incident and had the meteorite dug out of its hole, weighed and measured. Later, he admitted that although the stone had originally weighed 56 pounds, it was subsequently 'diminished in a small degree by different pieces being taken from it as presents to different literati of the country'. Expert analysis at the time described it as black, vitrified, and of volcanic origin, with the interior white, granulated, and very compact. They considered it as 'totally different from any kind of stone yet discovered'. The main bulk of the meteorite was given to the Natural History Museum, South Kensington, and Mr Topham erected the obelisk on the exact spot where it had fallen.

By now, the stream down the Wold Valley is officially recognised by the Ordnance Survey as the Gypsey Race – the 'G' is hard, incidentally. The name probably originates from the word 'geyser', itself derived from the Norse 'gypa' (a spring). Gypseys are streams which flow intermittently, fed by streams from the chalk of the Yorkshire Wolds which allows the formation of natural underground reservoirs. When the water table of these rises to a particular level, water is siphoned to the surface, oddly enough this occurring very often after a dry season rather than a wet one. Writing about 800 years ago, William of Newburgh was perhaps the earliest writer to refer to the strange nature of these streams: 'These famous waters, commonly called Vipseys, rise out of the ground from a number of springs, not indeed, continually, but every other year, and forming no small stream, run through the low ground to the sea. Their drying-up is a good sign, for their running is supposed a never-failing presage of famine.' Last year (1974) the Gypsey Race was not only quiescent but for long stretches non-existent, merely a dry channel. But then, it was rather a wet year!

Burton Fleming is the next village, well placed at the junction of six roads dipping slightly into the hollow where the brick cottages and farms of the eighteenth and nineteenth centuries group themselves to the south of the church and the manor house (now a farm). Queen Henrietta Maria is said to have stayed overnight here on her journey to York to join Charles I. Since Tudor times the village has also been called North Burton, and the map gives both names.

Two miles east is the lost village of Bartindale, which may

have become depopulated when Bardney Abbey acquired the lands for a sheep-walk, and probably established a grange there in the fifteenth century. Continuity of life (and farming) on the Wolds is typified here with a recent account of the history of Bartindale Farm, which was an entry for a farm history competition organised in 1968 by the *Farmers' Weekly*. It may well be that the present farm occupies the exact site of an Anglo-Saxon house, with successive rebuildings and alterations, the present brick structure being around 1800. Some of the boundary hedges of the farm run along raised banks and are not cut by any other hedges – signs of a great age, confirmed by their having between six and eight species of shrub in them, which dates them to 600–800 years ago. By contrast, the straight hedges are of hawthorn only and date from around 1773, when enclosures were made.

Nearby are the ancient earthworks of Argam Dikes, linear entrenchments which may be Iron Age boundaries, and the deserted village of Argam between Burton Fleming and Grindale, where cottages and farms are grouped about a pond, and a Roman building was discovered many years ago. The lane running south from the village takes us down to Boynton and the Gypsey Race again.

While we have been making this eastward journey along the Wold Valley by a quiet lane, a busier road, the B.1253, has been following a parallel course only two or three miles to the south, and 200 or 300 feet higher. A return to Sledmere can be made this way, detouring first to take in Thwing, quietly sat in a slight green hollow, with a reedy pond at its eastern end and a church on a bank at the other. This has an abnormally long squint between the end pier of the north aisle and the chancel, which necessitated building an extra bulge on the outside to accommodate it.

Langtoft is four miles to the south-west, a large red-roofed village extending along the B.1249 Driffield road and situated in an unusually deep hollow for a Wold village. Its two ponds were dry when I visited it, a contrast to some occasions in history, for on one of the brick houses in the centre of the village a plaque records a severe flood of the seventeenth century, and another in 1892 when there was a local waterspout. Indeed, close to the village, the sides of the chalk Wolds still bear the scars of the water channels which gushed down them, causing a seven-foot flood in Langtoft. Almost inevitably, the church is a Sir Tatton restoration, by Hodgson Fowler early this century. He also gave to the village a rather beautiful cross which now stands close to the smaller of the ponds.

A mile south-west along a lonely lane the grassy mounds and hummocks tell of another deserted village, Cottam, which was depopulated during the fifteenth and sixteenth centuries. Yet in early Victorian times, like so many Wold villages, there was a substantial increase in its population; indeed, an 1841 survey, showed that although there were only two inhabited farmsteads at Cottam, they housed 41 people, the explanation being that it was common practice to board on the farm all those people who worked there. Oddly enough, at Cowlam two miles away, site of another deserted medieval village, an almost identical circumstance occurred, with 44 inhabitants living in the two farmsteads. The church at Cowlam shelters behind a fine belt of trees, adjacent to a farmyard. Rebuilt last century it still has its high-backed pews, a two-decker pulpit, and a huge Norman font, peopled with a rare variety of carved figures. From Cowlam a minor road offers a pleasantly direct route back to Great Driffield.

CHAPTER EIGHT

Wolds, Central and Southern

Five miles east of the River Derwent at Stamford Bridge the Yorkshire Wolds present their steep scarp face to the west. The main road, the A.166, from York to Great Driffield and the coast urges you on across the Vale of York towards the crest of the hills ahead. Elms and oaks give way to beeches, a splendid avenue of them accompanying the north side of the road as it climbs deceptively steeply up the curving gradients of Garrowby Hill, with the highest point in the East Riding, 808 feet at Garrowby Top.

The steepness of the contours gives the impression of a greater height as well as the reward of a splendid view across the Vale. Garrowby Park, away to the north along the Wold edge, hides the Hall built by Tower in 1893 for the second Viscount Halifax in the style of two centuries earlier. Opposite, to the south of the main road, the slopes of North Cliff are sheep-grazed near the top, a foretaste of what is to come, and a piece of changeless Wold scenery evoking the past.

The busy A.166 is a good road to leave for the quieter lanes and fields of the central Wolds between it and the B.1246, Pocklington to Great Driffield road. Bishop Wilton is a mile south of the main road reached by a lane along the foot of the Wolds or a more attractive but hilly descent from near the top of Garrowby Hill. This drops you down into Bishop Wilton, past the site of the former summer palace of the archbishops, now a grassy platform and some mounds in a field.

The village is a delight. A stream flows down a grassy hollow between cottages set well back on each side, creating a feeling of space. Some modern in-filling is in harmony with the older brick houses, the green slopes of the Wolds making an ideal background to one of the most attractive of the East Riding villages. Behind the north side of the village, the church is one of J. L. Pearson's best pieces of restoration for Sir Tatton Sykes, carried out in 1858–9, and retains much good Norman work. Temple Moore's remarkable floor of 1902 is of black and white tiles in a pattern copied from one in the Vatican, mainly scrolls, but including about ten different species of birds repeated regularly throughout the whole floor area.

From Bishop Wilton a road leads southwards along the foot of the steeply-sloping Wolds, eventually reaching Pocklington. By turning left within a mile we can soon climb to the top of the Wolds again, first to Great Givendale, a hamlet with wooded hillsides curving away behind it, and tiny church nestling in a dip to the east of the village. The road to Millington continues south from Great Givendale before swinging eastwards to the village, sheltering under a west-facing slope of the Wolds north-east of Pocklington.

The green valley of Millington Beck fans out towards the Vale, and the situation of the village is more impressive than the place itself, but the little church has a Norman nave and chancel, with a west gallery. A splendidly scenic road runs along the brow of the western side of Millington Dale, which, like some of those around Thixendale, is too steep-sided to plough, so its character and scenery are probably very much as they were 200 years ago when most of the Wolds were unenclosed sheep-walks.

Millington Pastures were famous throughout the Wolds. The main field of over 400 acres was used as a common pasture of rich close-cropped grass sloping down sharply to a dry valley. All the farmers in the district shared it, each renting a number of 'gaits' or 'stints'. A gait represented pasturage for six sheep, or four sheep with their lambs, and Millington Pastures were shared into 108 gaits, controlled by the Pasture Master. Until recently the Pastures were a survival of the old way of open-pasture sheep-farming on the Wolds, but in the early 1960s they were eventually enclosed and sown with crops. Two public rights-of-way lead from the metalled road in Millington Dale, northwards to Millington Heights, one of the bridleways following the line of a Roman road we encountered earlier west of Thixendale. The site of a Roman villa was discovered nearby in 1745, with the remains of buildings, mosaic pavements, and some coins.

'Public Footpath' signs, offer encouragement to explore the Wolds here on foot, a surer way of capturing their essence, which was one of the reasons why the East Riding Area of the Ramblers' Association prepared a scheme in 1968 for the creation of a long-distance footpath to be called 'The Wolds Way'. By February 1971 the East Riding County Council had approved a route based on that originally suggested. Of its 67 miles from Filey Brigg to the Humber at North Ferriby, less than one third is on definitive rights-of-way, a quarter is on minor roads, and another quarter is on tracks which have not yet been legally approved.

The appeal of this part of the Wolds is in their simplicity of line and contour. Valleys are secretive, subtle in solitude, especially where they close in and their sides become progressively steeper. Few of them are named on the maps, but one which leads north from the end of the unfenced road up Millington Dale has a bridleway along its grassy bottom, a quiet invitation to a green and lonely paradise. By keeping to the road which continues to climb gently to the head of Millington Dale, you join another road which has come over Cold Wold from Warter. Near their junction another footpath leads to the edge of Millington Dale, giving a glorious view across the dale to Millington Pastures, a view of clean-lined horizons, distant squared fields, straight hedges, and spacious skies, with sheep grazing the dale slopes.

This is West Field, one of the open fields of Huggate, a mile to the east, where many of the minor Wold roads meet. Perhaps the most characteristic of all the Wolds villages, Huggate has no pretensions to great charm or beauty, but just sits there tucked away off the road, with most of its houses and farms close to a large village green where a well is reputed to be over 300 feet deep. The church stands at the northern end of the village and retains its fourteenth-century battlemented tower.

Travelling the Wold roads around Huggate emphasises the apparent loneliness of the landscape. Roadside farms are the exception; far more common are the isolated farms set well back down their own lanes, and usually sheltered by trees on three sides, and surrounded by their enclosed fields, a pattern set between 1770 and 1830.

Roads lead eastwards from Huggate, passing first the Wolds Inn with its attractively painted sign. The land drops gently in height as you travel to Tibthorpe and the B.1248, which forms a convenient limit to this exploration of the Wolds. We follow the good straight road for four miles south-east to North Dalton, where the main Pocklington–Great Driffield road, B.1246, passes a large pond where a single willow tree adorns a tiny island favoured by the resident duck population. High up on the opposite side of the road is the church, large, broad, with a Norman chancel arch and south door which has one capital having small busts beneath arches.

Two miles south the A.163 is encountered at Middleton-on-the-Wolds, where the main road sweeps down into a dip from both east and west. By the crossroads at the foot of the hill a well-kept green has seats thoughtfully placed on it, but no paths lead to them and a notice warns 'Keep off the Grass'. A large pond is adjacent to the green, with an attractive L-shaped range of white houses to the north. The church looks down on the village from its wooded knoll above the crossroads. Although much of the building is Victorian there is a fine thirteenth-century chancel with its inside walls of chalk, and lancet windows. A Norman tub font shows fleurs-de-lys and intersecting arches in its good quality decoration.

The main road seems to hurry you westwards on to the Wolds again, climbing the straight hill between the brick cottages and then crossing the course of the old railway line from Market Weighton to Great Driffield, a relatively recent link opened in 1890 as part of a system linking Scarborough and Bridlington with the West Riding.

Shelter-belts a mile long extend from Middleton Wold House to far beyond Kipling House, and presently a metalled road turns off northwards to Warter. Its opposite arm is a broad track, first chalky and then grassy, descending gradually to the south-east. This is the setting for the oldest horse race in England, the Kiplingcotes Derby, run every year on the third Thursday in March.

Tradition asserts that the race was first run in 1519, the date which is given on the winning-post by the side of the lane to Warter, but the first authentic record of the race puts it at 1555, when it was called Kibling Cotes. In his authoritative *Northern Turf History,* Major J. Fairfax Blakeborough writes that the Kiplingcotes Derby was founded in 1619, while in the *Topographical Dictionary of Yorkshire* of 1822, Thomas Langdale records the year as 1618, adding that the race was endowed by 'five noblemen, 19 baronets and 25 gentlemen of the county of Yorkshire'. Led by Lord Burlington, these 50 men contributed 360 shillings between them, the prize-money for the winner coming from the interest on this.

The race is open to horses of all ages, 'to carry horseman's weight, ten stones, exclusive of saddle, to enter at ye post, before eleven o'clock on the morning of ye race. The race to be run before two.' Its route covers about four miles and is mainly a rough track across fields, although it does end on the metalled road north of the A.163. Contrary to normal custom the weigh-in takes place by the winning-post where the rules are read by the hereditary clerk of the course. Should any rider find himself (or herself, as women have competed since 1933) under the approved ten stones, there is no shortage of flints in the adjacent fields with which to fill a bag to hang round the waist and thus tip the scales correctly.

There is little financial gain for the winner, since he only receives the interest on the original endowment, something between £15 and £20 nowadays. The second does much better, as he gets £4 out of each entry fee of £4.25, and as there may be at least ten or a dozen entries, he can expect £40 to £50. This leaves a few pounds only for the committee to pay any expenses, and makes Kiplingcotes Derby the most economically run race, as well as the oldest and strangest one in the country. On the remaining 364 days in the year, the track down the slope to the old Kiplingcotes Station is as pleasant a Wolds walk as you could wish for, with good woodlands both north and south. The station has a new lease of life as an antique shop.

Back on the main road, and heading south-west across Easthorpe Wold, height is gradually lost over the next couple of miles. By turning north at a crossroads the woods of Londesborough Park are soon recognized, although the house itself is hidden away to the north of the village. The road climbs past the entrance lodge of the park, with a lake close by and a public bridleway leads through part of the park to a corner of the village near the church.

Londesborough's history goes back to Roman times, and in 1895 traces of the Roman road from Malton to Brough were discovered at the bottom of the lake. Tradition suggests that Londesborough was also the site of a summer palace of the Kings of Northumbria, where Edwin met Paulinus before his conversion to Christianity. In the fifteenth century Londesborough came into the great north country family of the Cliffords, and then the estate passed by marriage to the earls of Burlington and then to the Cavendishes. It was the third earl who laid out the great park at Londesborough, giving it lakes, waterfalls, and terraces, and planted Londesborough Clump. A friend of artists and writers he was in his own right both a statesman and an architect, and after returning in 1715 from his Grand Tour in Italy he sponsored an English edition of Palladio, whose apostle he had become. There is a fine avenue of elms which he planted in memory of David Garrick, a frequent visitor to the house. It was during these visits that the parson used to ask the great actor for advice on reading the Scriptures in church.

Londesborough Hall passed to the Cavendishes and the sixth Duke of Devonshire pulled the house down in 1819. It is said that when he later visited the site of his destruction he 'shed tears over the ruin he had wrought'. No doubt the consolation of selling the 12,000 acre estate in 1845 for £470,000 would have helped to eradicate the memory of his misdeed. The buyer was George Hudson, who was planning the line from York to Market Weighton, and he routed it so that it passed the edge of the estate, where he built his own private station near the village of Shiptonthorpe, and created a two-mile drive through an avenue of trees from the house to the station. You can still look down this avenue from the roadside west of Londesborough, but Hudson's station has gone. Indeed, it was not many years before he left Londesborough, for his financial empire collapsed in 1849, and Albert Denison bought the estate. The first Lord Londesborough's wealth had arisen through banking, and he applied some of it to enlarging the estate. During their years at Londesborough the family became great figures in the racing world, but by 1937 when the earldom ended with the fourth earl's death, many thousands of acres of the estate had been sold.

Londesborough church is close to the park gates. The white limestone of its seventeenth-century south porch has been the target for initiallers of nearly three centuries, some of them being accompanied by identifiable dates from the 1690s to the 1870s. The sundial above is dated 1764, but in the tympanum above the Norman door is a fine eleventh-century Anglo-Danish cross-head. In the north chapel hang four banners which were carried at the funerals of the earls of Burlington, while in the chancel members of the family are commemorated by inscribed brass plates, the best being that of the architect earl. The almshouses to the west of the church, were founded in 1680 by the first earl, and consist of two groups of single-storey brick houses, each group built round three sides of a square.

The road northwards from Londesborough climbs up by what was one of the open fields of the village. On the Wold top it passes within a short distance of the huge Burnby Chalk Pit, one of the few quarries on the Wolds which is still being worked. The road drops sharply down to the little valley where shelters the straggling village of Nunburnholme, bordering a little chalk stream which flows by the roadside. Named after a long-vanished convent for Benedictine nuns, the village has many small and attractive cottages, white-walled and red-roofed, splashes of colour against the copse-dappled vale whose woods, trees, and hedges so greatly impressed the Reverend Francis Orpen Morris, the ornithologist, who was Rector here from 1854 until 1893. In the cream-washed rectory by the church he wrote his six-volume *History of British Birds* as well as numerous other books, including an encyclopedia of stately homes. His chief memorial is the church-tower which was rebuilt in 1901 to the design of Temple Moore, but retaining its richly-carved Norman arch. The small Norman nave is only 15 feet wide and has a Norman window and door in the north wall. Older than these, however, is the finest Anglo-Saxon cross in the East Riding, dating from *c*. 1000, and consisting of two joined fragments of the shaft. Although worn, its carving reveals many seated figures shown in profile, a Madonna and Child, and several animals.

From Nunburnholme a road threads its way up the valley past woodlands on either side, to the next village, Warter. The woods to the north form part of the park of Warter Priory. Again there are no traces of the original building founded in 1132 by Geoffrey Fitz Pain for Augustinian Canons. The present house is built on a late seventeenth-century centrepiece, with Victorian additions, and its 300-acre park has the head of Bielby Beck flowing through it, helping to create a lake.

Warter village lies in a wooded hollow, a situation best appreciated in the view from the south-east, where the extra height is sufficient to allow it to be seen, enfolded by Wolds pale with summer corn, dark with mature woodlands. The road from Great Driffield to Pocklington drops down past the trees and pond, and then climbs gently between the church and a triangular green with an unusually pleasing row of thatched houses with thatched porches and gabled windows.

The road to Pocklington passes through a dark tunnel of trees along the northern edge of the park of Warter Priory, climbs up to about 500 feet before descending to the edge of the beautiful estate of Kilnwick Percy, where a side road leads off by the lake to Kilnwick Percy Hall, and the few houses associated with it. The village name emphasises the extent to which the Percys held huge estates over the north of England, this one dating back to the thirteenth century.

On the eastern outskirts of Pocklington are the famous Burnby Hall Gardens, with one of the finest collections of water-lilies in Europe, the outcome of 30 years devoted attention by their creator, Major Percy Marlborough Stewart. A pioneer of travelling during the early years of motoring, between 1906 and 1920 he and his wife made eight car journeys round the world. He continued his travels until 1926 when he settled down in Pocklington, developed his gardens, and looked after his estates. Lakes were created, stocked with fish, and in 1935 planted with water-lilies, now numbering 50 varieties and totalling 5,000 plants. After Major Stewart's death in 1962 the local council bought the property as its administration centre, the gardens and the Stewart Collection being left to the people of Pocklington.

For centuries Pocklington has been one of the few important marketing centres for farmers from the Wolds. Like Beverley and Great Driffield it lies on the boundary between the chalk and the clay, sheltering at the foot of the Wold slopes to the north. To its broad squares and wide streets the seventeenth- and eighteenth-century farmers brought their produce and stock, obtaining from the town provisions and seeds, a pattern which continues today, but supplemented by newer industries. In 1743 its population was just under 1,000, but by the end of the century had risen to 1,500, and by 1850 to about 2,500, indicating a movement of people from the villages nearby to the town which served them.

By then it had been linked to York by the railway, and the Pocklington Canal was proving a reasonably successful commercial operation. A description in 1866 records that Pocklington had its regular Saturday market, four fairs a year, and that corn-milling, brewing, iron founding and the growing of flax were the main industries. Its large pedimented methodist church had just been built, and still stands proudly in a pleasant group with a minister's house on each side. Three other chapels, as well as the parish church, a grammar school, national school, and workhouse made up the other main build-

129

ings in the town.

The boldly handsome Perpendicular tower of the parish church still dominates the town, and stands fair comparison with that at Great Driffield. Most of the church is late twelfth to late thirteenth-century, and the transepts contain a number of good monuments.

Pocklington School occupies a long ivy-covered building by West Green, near the line of the railway. Founded by John Dolman in 1514 as a 'fraternity' comprising a master, two wardens, with a number of brothers and sisters, the foundation included lands in Yorkshire and Derbyshire, income from which would enable five scholars from the school to go to St John's College, Cambridge. In 1552 the endowment of the school was transferred to the college, a patronage which was removed in 1875 when Pocklington School became the responsibility of its own governing body. 1944 saw it become a direct grant school and it now has over 600 boys, of which about half are boarders coming from all over England and from abroad.

The building of Pocklington Canal was a purely local project, the Act permitting it was passed in 1815 and the canal opened in July 1818, having cost £32,000, less than the estimate of its engineer, George Leather. Linking Pocklington with the navigable River Derwent, its nine-mile course included nine locks, eight swing bridges, and four brick bridges. It was used chiefly to carry agricultural products to the expanding industrial towns of the West Riding, and to bring back coal, lime, fertilisers and various industrial goods. After 30 years of steady trade it was bought by the York and North Midland Railway, later the L.N.E.R. Inevitably, maintenance deteriorated so that by the end of the century trade had almost ceased, although it was not until 1932 that the last commercial boat sailed up it, and the last pleasure boat two years later.

Now, there is every hope that it may be revived as an amenity waterway and linear leisure park. In 1969 the Pocklington Canal Amenity Society was formed with these aims. Enthusiastic working parties have cleared towpaths, cleaned out lock chambers, and repaired brickwork. Fund-raising activities have been augmented by local authority help, and in 1971 Cottingwith Lock was reopened; trailed boats can already use parts of the canal, while the towpath is mostly in good enough order to be regularly used by anglers and the general public.

Canal Head is by the A.1079 a mile south of Pocklington, and opposite 'The Wellington Oak', but no terminal buildings survive, apart from a barn which was originally a warehouse. There are five locks in the first two miles to the first road bridge near Bielby. This, like the next two at Walbut and Thornton, each with its lock, is characteristic of the canal's splendid brick bridges. Wide road approaches curve elegantly inwards to the humped, narrow apex, most noticeable on Church Bridge at Thornton. Each bridge has four semi-circular buttresses on each side.

West of Thornton Lock the canal passes Melbourne, where there is a side-arm as at Bielby. Three miles farther on, Hagg Bridge carries the B.1228 York road over the canal, which then swings southwards to join the tidal Derwent beyond Cotting-with Lock. Throughout its course the canal has obtained its water from the nearby beck, a factor which, allied to its scenic value and enthusiastic amenity group, may help to secure its use as a pleasant East Riding waterway before the end of this decade.

Between Market Weighton and Londesborough in the shallow gap separating the Central Wolds from those to the south, is the village of Goodmanham. It was described by the Venerable Bede as 'this one-time place of idols, . . . called today Godmundingaham . . . ' – a reference to the occasion when King Edwin and his high priest Coifi were converted from their pagan beliefs by the great missionary Paulinus. Their heathen temple is supposed to have occupied the site of the present church which is mainly Norman, with the most decorative fonts in the East Riding, nearly five feet high on its short stem, with a deep bowl richly carved all over its eight sides. Its fifteenth-century splendour contrasts with its smaller Norman companion. The church stands centrally in the village with attractive groups of houses around it, the best being Hall Garth, originally the rectory of 1823, a two-storeyed five-bay building of pale yellow brick, with a Doric portico.

Four miles from Goodmanham, Holme-on-the-Wolds is a hamlet just off the main B.1248 Beverley – Wetwang road while to the south the splendid spire of South Dalton church is a landmark for many miles around this eastern edge of the Wolds, where the land has gradually decreased in height. 'A superb Pearson steeple', Pevsner describes it, all 200 feet, very slender and with four pinnacles keeping close to it. The church itself dates from 1858–61, built by the third Baron Hotham at a cost of £25,000, in Pearson's best thirteenth-century High Gothic, with nave, transepts and chancel culminating in a magnificent sanctuary and an impressive east window.

South Dalton has absorbed its neighbouring village of Holme-on-the-Wolds into the one parish of Dalton Holme, and the chancel of the old church at Holme now stands a roofless, ivy-covered ruin in a field. The village of South Dalton is down the street from the church, with a row of nineteenth-century almshouses closest to the church. Beyond it, on the other side of the road, a seventeenth-century half-timbered house is probably the oldest in the village, most of which seems to have been laid out as an estate village in the eighteenth and nineteenth centuries. Plenty of splendid trees help to create both shelter and a sense of unity, especially where a road turns off westwards towards the entrance to the park, continuing through the lodge gates as a public highway to South Dalton Wold and Kiplingcotes Farm, and then following the line of the old railway to Market Weighton.

Mature beeches in groups and avenues grace the 400-acre parkland, with the fine house of Dalton Hall occupying higher ground to the south. Thomas Atkinson designed the house for the Hothams in 1771–5: a rather austere building in grey brick, but the adjacent stable-block is mid-nineteenth-century, although its inner courtyard seems to be contemporary with Dalton Hall itself. Some distance away to the west is the Summer House, supposedly designed by Colen Campbell, and similar to his former gateway to Burlington House, with four rusticated columns and a pediment over the large entrance arch.

Two miles south Etton is an attractive street village of the usual eighteenth- and nineteenth-century houses along both sides of the road, with the pond an important feature near the middle of the village. The church dominates the eastern end of the village from its situation on a green bankside. Although largely rebuilt about the middle of last century, much genuine Norman work survives, in the lower part of the tower, in its south and west windows, and most impressively in its tower arch. Immediately below and to the south of the church is the remarkably neat group of village school and house adjoining, brick, with beautifully kept gardens.

More splendid trees are at Cherry Burton, a large village a mile to the south. Oaks and beeches, elms and yews adorn the park that surrounds the hall, and in the village itself the brick-built and red-tiled cottages of the past two centuries are a foil for their modern counterparts. New estates of good quality houses built in the traditional styles emphasise the nearness of Cherry Burton to Beverley and even to Hull itself. The old smithy with the pond nearby may be of the old order; the garage and the busy B.1248 are of more relevance to the commuter, and the villages on these eastern edges of the Wolds offer desirable dormitory prospects.

From Cherry Burton a lane leads southwards to its more famous neighbour on the main road, Bishop Burton, passing on its way the grounds of the East Riding College of Agriculture. The estate, which now covers 670 acres, was bought by the County Council in 1953, and has been gradually added to since then. With 570 acres used as arable and grassland, the College and its farms provide a wide range of courses in agriculture, always having the essential ingredient of plenty of practical instruction for the many students of both sexes who are accommodated at the College.

This northern way into Bishop Burton does not prepare you for its rather self-conscious beauty. The village could doubtless hold pride of place in any East Riding competition. Its southerly approach from Walkington, or the more usual one by the main road from Market Weighton coming down from Cherry Burton Wold into the wooded hollow that quietly holds Bishop Burton, these lead you more gently to the crescent-shaped village pond. Chestnut trees are dotted around a spacious, well-kept green on the opposite side of the main road, and the green narrows to an apex at its northern end, flanked by cottages, with a smaller pool, reed-fringed, which mirrors the white-washed walls and pantiles of the house close by.

Behind the trees the low west tower of the church stands sturdily on its mound site, well above the village roofs. Although a few Norman fragments survive, there has been much rebuilding, including a chancel in Pearson's Early English style, 1865. There are some good brasses of the fifteenth and sixteenth centuries, and more unusually, a bust of John Wesley in the vestry. This was carved from the trunk of an elm which formerly graced the village green, which tree apparently sheltered Wesley during a visit here.

I think that he would approve of the open-air service held on the green each year on a Sunday afternoon in late July. This idea was first tried out in 1965 and has now become a well-attended event, perhaps its greatest attraction being that the music is provided by a splendid fairground organ powered by a shining steam traction engine. The melodies of well-known hymns have a certain unorthodoxy of chord and tempo, but their tone, duly amplified by a congregation of over 200 in summer attire (my visit was on a warm sunny day), sounds right in this exquisite rural setting.

Westwards, the main road to Market Weighton, although reaching no great height, nevertheless gives the impression of a lonely route through a vast and open landscape. North and south are extensive views of summer cornfields, cloud-dappled, or in another season grey-brown with the newly-turned soil, when the beech-clumps and shelter-belts are dark in winter. Near the top of the Wold, Arras lies just north of the main road. The farm with a few cottages may once have been an ancient demesne having a lot of land but no enclosures or fences except for small ones near the buildings. In the early nineteenth century it was surrounded by about 20 square miles of open fields, mainly sheep-walks, rabbit warrens and some cornfields. There is no record of any full enclosures being made, yet by 1840 the process had been completed, and Arras Farm then owned 900 acres in this depopulated township.

Tumuli and barrows speak of ancient occupation of the Wolds above Market Weighton. The broad road sweeps down towards the little town on a gradient which looks insignificant but which has justified the building of a length of escape road as it enters the built-up area, to halt any heavy goods vehicles which may have lost control.

A little chalk stream flows down from the Wolds near Goodmanham to meet the flat claylands of the broad Vale of Derwent. Market Weighton developed as a pleasant, placid market town by this stream and just to the west of the Roman road from Brough to Malton. When, by 1765, the road from York to Beverley had been turnpiked through the town, crossing the old road from Goole to Great Driffield, Market Weighton's importance increased, but never to such an extent that it became a busy agricultural centre.

That same York–Beverley turnpike is now the A.1079, a busy, noisy trunk road with all that means to an otherwise quiet country town. With no narrow streets or awkward corners to negotiate, traffic seems to surge through so that crossing the main road in the town can be distinctly hazardous. Yet there are quiet corners, particularly to the north of the main road and behind the church, where Church Lane and The Green show some attractive corners. The former police station is by The Green, dated 1843, a neat little building of typical East Riding pattern, with small late Georgian brick houses nearby. Contrasting with the small houses is a huge nineteenth-century warehouse occupying most of the centre of the area between The Green and Church Lane, and behind the yard of the Londesborough Arms, whose impressive frontage and heraldic sign make the best façade in the main street.

Market Weighton's parish church of All Saints is prominent if not architecturally outstanding. It has some eleventh-century herring-bone masonry on the arcade, whose walls, like those of the chancel, are coldly white. One of the many monuments commemorates William Bradley, who died in 1820 aged 33. Measuring 7ft 9ins tall and weighing 27 stones, this Yorkshire giant made a fortune in the show-business world of fairground freaks and appeared in most towns in England.

Near the road junction at the west end of the main street stands the large uninteresting methodist church. In the adjoining yard is its little predecessor of 1786, where Wesley preached. This is now used as a furniture store, but not used at all is the once-handsome railway station of 1848, by Andrews.

George Hudson had opened his line from York to Market Weighton in 1847, but it was not until 1865 that it was extended to link up with the Hull–Bridlington line near Beverley. Meanwhile, in 1848, a branch from Selby to Market Weighton was opened, bringing more trade to the town, whose station must have been one of the most impressive in Yorkshire. Stone-built of eleven bays and paired Tuscan columns it was proudly classical. Now it is derelict, and dismal, its windows broken, its masonry despoiled or decaying, its surroundings forlorn and sad.

The Wolds become narrower as they edge towards the Humber a few miles west of Hull. Their western limit is very nearly followed by the A.1034 running south from Market Weighton, by way of the Newbalds and the Caves to join the main trunk road, the A.63, curving eastwards to within a few hundred yards of the river. Meanwhile, south from Beverley, the A.164 forms a convenient eastern boundary to this small area of the Wolds lying south of the main Market Weighton–Beverley road. Most of the villages to be visited lie close to these main roads, with only Little Weighton and Walkington situated more aloofly within the triangle, and the higher land towards its west.

A journey down the main road from Market Weighton towards the Humber retains the essential flavour of the Wolds for many miles. The Roman road from Lincoln to York came this way: so did John Wesley, who, at the age of 85, preached in Sancton Church on Monday 23 June 1788, at nine o'clock in the morning. The old man had preached twice at Hull the day before, and from Sancton he went on to preach at Market Weighton at eleven, Pocklington at two, and at York in the evening. Six services in two days and many miles of travel on horseback, shows a selfless energy which may have shamed the easy-going parsons of the established church, and no doubt helped to inspire the building of the scores of angular, ugly, Primitive Methodist chapels characteristic of so many villages of the East Riding.

The beautiful tower of Sancton Church is the Riding's only one which is octagonal throughout its complete height. Although the church was rebuilt 1869–71, the fifteenth-century tower is unspoilt, with its lantern top and pinnacles crowning the buttresses. The Langdales have held estates near Sancton since before Norman times, and Sir Marmaduke is commemorated by a simple stone in the church, 1661. A century later, Philip Langdale built Houghton Hall, west of Sancton, to designs by Atkinson. A glimpse of the house can be obtained from across the large lake to its south, and part of Thomas White's landscaped park of 1768.

North and South Newbald lie in a hollow of the Wolds just east of the Beverley road, the former being the major settlement; an attractive cluster of cottages, grey stone or whitewashed, around an irregular green north of the church. North Newbald church is one of the few within the East Riding which is built of an oolitic limestone. Local quarries were worked as long ago as the thirteenth century, and some of the stone for Beverley Minster came from them. The pale honey-coloured church is the most complete Norman building in the East Riding, cruciform and without aisles, flat-buttressed, with round-arched windows and four Norman doorways – north and south ones into the nave and north and south ones into the respective transepts.

More of North Newbald village lies to the east of the church, along the lanes which climb steadily on to the clean open landscape of Newbald Wold. Again, there is no great height, but the spaciousness is there. One lane forks off north to Newbald Lodge and Cherry Burton Wold; another continues eastwards, passing few farms and no villages until Beverley is reached almost eight miles away. The other lane from North Newbald tops the 500 foot contour by High Hunsley, where it crosses the B.1230 Beverley road and continues to Little Weighton, a quietly unassuming village of no outstanding attractions.

A mile to its south-west, however, is Rowley, where a glance at the map is sufficient to indicate something out of the ordinary. The road appears to head directly for the church in its parkland setting, but swings suddenly to the south, almost following the edge of the park round three sides of a hexagon before returning to its original alignment. When the roads were re-built at the time of the enclosures, the glebe lands of Rowley rectory remained sacrosanct, so although a public right-of-way exists to the church from both directions, the road has taken its more circuitous course to the south since the eighteenth century. The rectory, now an hotel, is early eighteenth-century, and on the well-kept lawn between the rectory and Rowley church is a most elegant little rotunda with Ionic columns supporting a dome of wrought iron.

In the early seventeenth century the rector of Rowley disagreed with the playing of any Sunday games, and refused to read in church the Book of Sports. As a result of his Puritanical opposition he was turned out of his living, so the Reverend Ezekiel Rogers not only decided to emigrate to America with all his possessions, but persuaded 20 local families to sail with him. They arrived in Massachusetts in 1638 and founded a new colony to which they gave the name of Rowley, now a thriving settlement called Rowley Burgh.

The little church is reached by a woodland path. It seems to belong to the garden of Rowley Manor, and there are roses growing around it. Cement-rendering of its walls detracts from its appearance without disguising its mainly Perpendicular style, with an older west tower. Inside, the most outstanding feature is the south chapel which dates from 1730 when Ellerker Bradshaw built it as a mausoleum to perpetuate the memory of the old family of Ellerker, of which many generations are commemorated.

West of Rowley four roads lead down from the Wolds to the series of villages between the Newbalds and North Ferriby, each accessible from the crossroads by Riplingham House – to South Cave, Brantingham, Elloughton and Welton. The most northerly of these roads crosses Cave Wold with its woodland landmark of Beverley Clump, and opposite it The Warrens suggests a former use of these sheep pastures and cornlands.

Beech plantations are very extensive along these western edges of the Wolds where they follow the contours, darkening the skyline from the descending roads, and for the most part dating from the late eighteenth century.

South Cave's boundaries extend from the chalk Wolds to the floor of the clay vale, giving the useful and characteristic variation in land use; pasture and arable on the top, arable below, with meadow and pasture occupying the lowest lands. The present village extends along arms of the four roads which cross here, the main road from Market Weighton coming down the hill to join the A.63 trunk road to Hull just south of the village. Houses, inns and Market Hall, all of them late eighteenth-century, face one another, the Market Hall, grey brick and with a cupola above its two storeys, proudly bearing its date, 1796, and less prominently beneath its open arcading, some old meat-hooks.

Much of South Cave lies along the road leading to its near neighbour, North Cave. Behind its high wall and wooded grounds the 1804 Gothic castle of yellow brick, turreted, battlemented, tall-chimneyed, is now a country club, its gatehouse at the west an 1870 addition and competing with the church for pride of place in the western approach to South Cave. The church, on a slight rise and screened by trees, has been locked on the occasions I have visited it.

The road continues westwards to North Cave, basically a street village with some good brick houses of the eighteenth and nineteenth centuries. A few of these at the west end of the village have particularly attractive doorways with simple Tuscan columns, and small pediments above. Nearby is a cast-iron milestone set into a mountingblock, and along the 'back lane' to the north of the main street brick gives way to stone. Lacking the heavy traffic of its neighbour, North Cave is a far more pleasant place in which to wander. Contributing to this fact is its nearness to Hotham Park, whose woodlands reach southwards to the village, with the church of North Cave at the corner. A large building of rubble with a partially Norman tower, its most peculiar feature is the absence of any arches across either the north or the south transepts so that the space they occupy is more like a double, or even triple, cube room.

Adjacent to the church is Hotham Estate Manor Farm (East) forming a good group, the farmhouse of 1770 facing its two yards with stables and cowsheds separating them, the central range of these including a neat eighteenth-century dovecote complete with cupola. Castle Farm is farther east again, another late eighteenth-century building which originally had castellations to make it an eyecatcher in the view from Hotham Hall. A public footpath follows the western edge of the parkland from North Cave to Hotham village, and passes closer to Hotham Hall than do any of the roads. Large Victorian glazed porches hide three of the ground-floor five bays of this 1683 house built for George Meltham in brown stones which are little larger than bricks. In the eighteenth century a three-bay pavilion was added to one side, and compensating extensions to the other, but the whole lacks a degree of unity.

Much of Hotham, which runs more or less as a single street north from the Hall to the church, seems to be an estate type of village with many attractive groups of houses, some of stone, with the church occupying a prominent site, guarded by tall elms, and with a red-roofed nave almost as high as its squat tower. This contains some Norman carving, and it is likely that the tower arch may have once been the chancel arch.

After this small detour involving the Caves and Hotham it is time to return to the main road, A.1034, and its Humber-wards alignment. In fact, if we go right back to the top of Cave Wold, almost to the crossroads at Riplingham we can then take the road signposted 'Brantingham'. This will soon bring us down the lovely, wooded Brantingham Dale, the most popular valley within easy reach of Hull, which is only ten miles away to the east. Coming off the open Wold its steep sides clothed with fine trees create a satisfying contrast which is lost if you explore the dale starting from its lower end. The route of the Wolds Way follows the valley road down through the woods for about a mile. Where the trees end, the church stands, some distance away from the village it serves, better in its situation than its architecture, a rebuilding by Street, 1872, for Sir Christopher Sykes.

Top: left (23) bench-end of jester from Hemingborough church; *right* (24) 12th-century Viking boat detail on south door, Stillingfleet church. *Bottom: left* (25) misericord in south-west stall at Hemingborough, c. 1200 and probably the earliest in England; *right* (26) misericord (c. 1425) in stalls of St Mary's, Beverley.

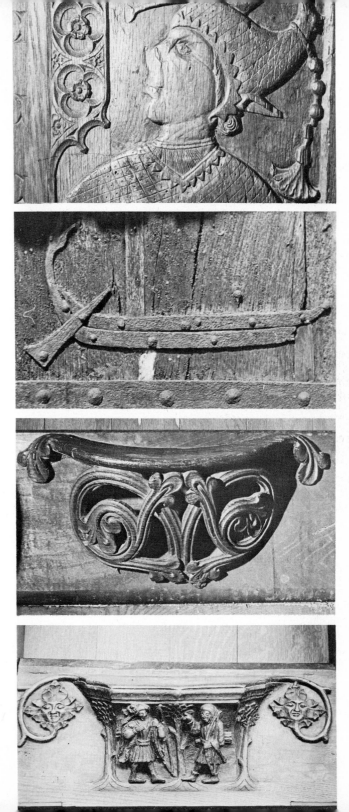

Half a mile away in the middle of Brantingham village is the Gothic war memorial built of stones taken from Hull's Town Hall of 1862. Pevsner describes it as 'lovably awful', and points out that the sundry urns scattered around the village are from the same source. I am not sure that Hull's loss was Brantingham's gain. On the tiny central bit of green where roads meet, is an old cast-iron pump, proud on its brick plinth with four concrete steps leading up to it. Such a focal point in an attractive village scene is a natural site for official additions so it has a large 'Keep Left' sign adjacent to it, and a power pole equally close. Thus is successfully tarnished the beauty of line and form and texture which the years have given to Brantingham. The cottages in the village try to compensate, and their wooden porches add a distinctively rustic touch. Brantingham Hall is a tall red-brick house by the village pond, five bays with a single pediment, and nearby is Thorpe Hall, a Victorian rebuilding of an older house, with fine gardens and lawns from which, it is said, both York Minster and Lincoln Cathedral can be seen. Wellingtonias have been planted in the grounds to commemorate various royal visits to the house.

Parallel valleys lead down from the Wolds one and two miles east of Brantingham Dale to Elloughton and Welton respectively. Elloughton Dale has a road along it, but the road into Welton follows the edge of the woodland and the Wold. From the heads of both dales there are fine views southwards across the busy Humber to the Lincolnshire Wolds; but the A.63 trunk road scything towards Hull marks the effective limit of the chalk country. Fortunately, it has been routed to by-pass Elloughton, Welton and Melton, so that these villages can retain something of a village character. Of them Welton claims pride of place, a remarkably attractive and unified village for one so close to the mawing grasp of Hull. It would certainly be included in my 'top ten' East Riding villages.

Where the chalk meets the clay at the foot of Welton Dale a series of springs feed into a long pond, frequented by geese and ducks, with Welton High Mill just downstream. The water subsequently flows clear and sparkling through the middle of the village, immediately north of the church, then broadening

27. The south front of Burton Agnes Hall, c. 1601–10, showing the very early bow windows extending a full three storeys.

into an ornamental pond with willows. The outflow from the pond takes it underground, but a large open green is more than adequate compensation for the loss of the stream. Sir Giles Gilbert Scott restored the church in 1862–3, and six of the windows have glass by Morris, the earlier ones of the 1870s being the better. Outside the east end is the headstone to Jeremiah Simpson bearing these words:

Here lyeth He ould
Jeremy who hath
eight times married
been but now in his
ould age he lies
in his cage under
The grass so green.

He died in 1719 in the 84th year of his age. Attractive houses line the green, and a group of eighteenth- and nineteenth-century ones occupy an island site to the south-west of the church. Beyond them, at the lower west end of the green is the white-fronted Green Dragon Inn, supposed to have been a favourite haunt of John Palmer, better known as Dick Turpin, and the place where he was eventually captured. An early nineteenth-century stone pump is a focal point between the church and the inn.

East of the green are Welton Hall and Welton Manor, late eighteenth-century, but earlier in date and hiding behind a high wall is Welton Grange. Unusually in a district where brick is predominant, this house is of stone and was probably built for a Hull merchant about the middle of the eighteenth century. Another fine house, Welton House, has recently been demolished. It was once the home of the Raikes family, who are commemorated by a mausoleum standing near the head of Welton Dale. Robert Raikes built this structure in 1818, a large round building 38 feet high, in the classical style and with a domed roof. After suffering some damage from vandals it is now in a better state of repair. The road leaving the eastern end of Welton village leads to Melton, where a left turn takes you past a huge quarry to Swanland, continuing into the outer suburbs of Hull at Kirk Ella, where there is an unusually splendid church with an eight-pinnacled tower and an array of excellent monuments. The old houses of the village are around the church, with a timber-framed one to its west, and eighteenth-century Wolfreton Hall on the south. Like so many villages close to Hull, the surviving older parts manage to retain some of their former character and dignity against the thrust of new housing estates and fast urban roads, one of which, the A.164 leads northwards towards more open countryside.

Soon, the windmill at Skidby appears on the skyline, the only working one in the East Riding. This tower mill dates from 1821 and was maintained in working order until after the last war by the Thompson family who owned it. In 1968, Mr Garfield Weston, of the milling family, presented the building to the Beverley Rural District Council, and they have restored it, and open it to the public on Saturdays. Dominating its adjoining group of brick single-storey farm buildings, Skidby Mill is black-tarred, with its four sails and window frames white, and an elegant white-painted ogee cap topped by a ball finial. Its fantail provides a graceful foil to the great sails, the whole structure a superb landmark on this south-eastern edge of the Wolds.

Skidby itself is west of the mill and off the main road, very much a street village with church and forge close to the small green. The road through the village continues to Little Weighton where another turns off northwards for Walkington, passing Risby Park on the way.

This southern approach from the Wolds leads directly to the church at Walkington, on the hillside above the village. A flight of four steps descends from the north door into the nave and another flight of four climbs up to the font beneath the sixteenth-century west tower, but the main focus of attention is the modern east window, a fiery array of vivid and sparkling colour, lively, vital and beautiful. A field-path from the church is a parallel but pleasanter way than the road by which to drop down to the village, where, along the one main street, plenty of good eighteenth- and nineteenth-century houses line the broad green verge in colourful harmony. Over the last few years there has been a lot of good restoration and modern integration, with the result that Walkington has appreciably grown without a deterioration of character and appearance. Even the village pond has been elongated and islanded. It, too, has a sanctuary cross by the roadside east of the village, a grey stone fragment of the original which marked the limit of sanctuary of Beverley Minster. The main road eastwards from Walkington enters Beverley by the golf course on Beverley Pastures, passing the stark, black-walled tower of the old windmill. This road, like its most important counterpart from Market Weighton, must offer one of the finest approaches to any town in England, even one so beautiful as Beverley itself.

CHAPTER NINE

Beverley to Great Driffield

In 1965, when the Council for British Archaeology published its promised list of British towns whose historic quality required most careful treatment in planning or redevelopment, 51 towns were regarded as having special importance. Four of these were in Yorkshire, Beverley, Richmond, Scarborough and York itself. There never could have been much doubt about Beverley's inclusion, for not only does it have its magnificent Minster and St Mary's Church, but scores of superb secular buildings from medieval times to the early nineteenth century. Another priceless asset is that it is ringed on three sides by common pastures which account for almost half the land area of the borough. They give the town its superb parkland setting covering two square miles, best appreciated by the western approach from York. As the last ridge of chalk is surmounted beyond Bishop Burton the rich green area of trees and fields which is Westwood rides the crest of the pastures, against which, in the distance, the towers of Beverley Minster gleam silvery-white in a westering sun.

This same ridge-top view must have greeted the earlier pilgrims to the sacred shrine of St John of Beverley. Having passed one of the sanctuary crosses they may have knelt and prayed in thanksgiving for their safe journey. Now, to the south of the road near Beverley Race Course the oaks and beeches of Burton Bushes are a survival of the ancient Westwood itself. Covering 640 acres, Westwood, with Hurn adjoining it on the north, is the biggest of the pastures, as well as the most attractive and popular. Archbishop Neville, a friend of Richard II, granted it to the town in 1380 at a burgage rent of 100 shillings, which is still paid. An earlier archbishop of York, Thurstan, who had granted Beverley its first charter in 1129, had also provided the first of the pastures, while others were given later by various Lords of the Manor. As they were all granted in perpetuity they remain as common-land for the townsfolk of Beverley for ever.

Beverley Pastures are controlled by 12 Pasture Masters who are elected annually on 1 March by the freemen of the town who are qualified as such by having reached the age of 21, and were either born in Beverley or have served a five-year apprenticeship with a freeman in the borough.

All the freemen have grazing rights on the pastures for one gait (pasturage for one cow, or three ewes with lambs); the remaining gaits are sold first to the freemen and then to nonfreemen, who pay about twice as much for a gait, putting their animals out to graze a week later (1st May) than the more privileged ones. Westwood alone has 450 gaits, and at its western end a pair of sheepdogs on wandering leads ensure that stock do not come out of the common by the main road, and probably do the job far better than a modern cattle-grid would do.

The common pastures give Beverley its setting, the Minster gives it grace. Yet, beautiful though it is, the Minster does not dominate the town but stands almost to one side, fronted on the south by a field, opposed on the north by elegant and narrow streets of eighteenth-century brick houses. Because it is away from the centre of the town Beverley Minster is not always the first building to be visited, although it is the oldest structure. Bede tells us that it was St John of Beverley who built the first church here in 690, soon to be ransacked by the Danes and then refounded by Athelstan as a collegiate church; its association with St John making it a place of pilgrimage as well as sanctuary. As a result, a small town grew to the north of the Minster, largely under its control, until Edward VI dissolved the college in 1547 and annexed its estates.

Meanwhile, the 1129 charter gave Beverley burgesses a

number of privileges and rights, so that by the end of the fourteenth century it had become famous for its wool trade. In 1334 it appears fifteenth in a list of provincial towns; by 1377 it had risen to tenth on the basis of its taxpaying population, above both Newcastle and Canterbury. By the sixteenth and seventeenth centuries its importance had gone, the wool trade had declined, and prosperity was falling, in spite of the granting in 1573 by Queen Elizabeth of its charter of incorporation. It never decayed; indeed, in the eighteenth century it flourished again, but by 1780 Hull was becoming the attraction for the new craftsmen of industry and the trades associated with shipping. The Regency period saw the building of some terraces along the edges of the pastures, and in late Victorian times a much greater concentration of terrace-housing was added, indistinguishable from similar areas in almost any of the growing towns of the nineteenth century.

Because the shape of Beverley was dictated by its surrounding fields, and the River Hull to the east, its present plan was developed during those early centuries of growth. A good supply and variety of building materials have contributed to the harmony of Beverley's buildings – timber from the Wolds and the lowlands, brick-clay from the numerous good deposits nearby, sand and gravel from alluvial deposits, chalk for mortar, and limestone from quarries at North Cave and Tadcaster brought by water. Ecclesiastical patronage has ensured no shortage of craftsmen working in these materials, a situation subsequently utilised by the wealthy cloth merchants who had their houses built in the sixteenth and seventeenth centuries. All these factors have contributed to the organic growth of Beverley that makes it such a visual delight, in spite of its battle against the chrome shop-front, the supermarket, the garage and the traffic.

The road from York leads directly to North Bar, the only survivor of the five town gateways. Beverley was never walled, although some early attempts to seek permission to fortify it are on record. At North Bar, the York Road meets the road from Driffield. North Bar Without, this is called, a delightful, tree-lined highway with greens and graciousness of Georgian houses, especially on its eastern side.

North Bar was built of bricks between 1409 and 1410 at a cost of £97 17s 4½d, and embodying at least 125,000 bricks made locally, and like most early bricks, irregular in form and size. The centuries have darkened them to a warm reddish-brown, seen best in evening when sunlight textures them, and highlights the edges of the three blind windows with cusped ogee heads which with the string course above makes this north face of Beverley's North Bar one of the most detailed examples of early brickwork in England.

Through the gateway is North Bar Within, a good terrace of late eighteenth-century three-storey houses. Beyond them, on the corner of Tiger Lane, is the best example of a half-timbered house with a good jettied overhang of the fifteenth century. But the great glory of this street is St Mary's, one of England's most beautiful parish churches, its white magnesian limestone having been brought from the quarries near Tadcaster. Because it is constricted by its situation at a street corner, St Mary's turreted Perpendicular west front almost wholly obscures the view of the tower from the main road, so that to see this it is necessary to continue past the junction of Wood Lane and look back to the church from the south-west. The tower collapsed in 1520, and was rebuilt almost immediately, crowned with battlements and a full array of sixteen pinnacles. What does surprise in this exterior view is the knowledge that the flying buttresses of the south transept are not medieval but a Victorian addition by the Pugins, father and son, who were carrying out a critical restoration of the church around 1850.

St Mary's had been built originally as a chapel-of-ease to the Minster, but it soon became the parish church of the craftsmen and merchants of the town. Fifteen separate stages of its building are recorded, starting in 1120 and ending with the rebuilding of the tower, with most of the work coming after 1280. Entry through the elegant south porch reveals an extremely rich interior, spacious and light with large clerestory windows. Evidence of the townspeople's contribution to the church building is nicely illustrated by the various inscriptions on the pillars of the north arcade. One particularly famous one has high up on the corbels and just below the capitals a quintet of little stone musicians in colourful Tudor costume looking down on the Sunday congregations.

A beautiful chapel occupies the north chancel aisle, with a sacristy attached to it, and a spiral staircase of diminishing diameter leads up to the so-called Priest's Room which may have been a former library or treasury. The misericords of the choir stalls, dating from 1425–50 show a wonderful array of subjects – knights, monks, green men and kings contrast with foxes, monkeys, an eagle, a boar, a pelican and a wyvern.

On the opposite corner of Hengate from St Mary's is the first of the many Georgian shop-fronts which grace the centre of Beverley. From North Bar Within, the road soon divides, part of it broadening out into Saturday Market, the traditional rectangular market place, narrowing at the farther end, with its area broken by island blocks of buildings. Focal point is the Market Cross, square, with slightly canted corners each having a pair of Tuscan columns capped by stone vases above the frieze. A good inscription tells us that the cross was erected at the expense of two local M.P.'s Sir Charles Hotham and Sir Michael Warton in 1714, the design being by Sheltan of Wakefield.

The best Georgian shop-fronts are on the east side of Saturday Market, earlier ones square-bowed, later ones slightly rounded. Too many modern facias overpower these older elegances, particularly along The Dings, near the Market Cross. However, the variety of shops, with some larger houses and inns, together with the Corn Exchange and the banks, certainly ensure a diversity of façade and roof-line. The nature of the trades for which the Saturday Market shops cater reflects Beverley's regional importance as an agricultural market town in an area famous for horses.

At its southern end Saturday Market narrows into Toll Gavel and then Butcher Row, culminating in the small triangle of Wednesday Market. By now, houses outnumber shops, and along Highgate, which leads to the Minster, a good terrace of small Georgian brick houses serves as a prelude to the soaring towers at its southern end. But before dealing with the Minster we must go back to Saturday Market and approach it another way. Lairgate is the alternative fork from North Bar Within, running west of Saturday Market. Part of a one-way traffic system, it has a number of large Georgian houses and hotels, and in the side road to the west, Newbegin, some of the best houses in Beverley. Newbegin House on the north side, of seven bays and a hipped roof was built for Charles Warton around 1690. Back in Lairgate, eighteenth and nineteenth century are represented best in its northern half, but if we continue down the street to the end, we turn left into Keldgate which takes us directly to the Minster. Inevitably, it seems, more eighteenth-century houses, with the fine range of Ann Routh's almshouses of 1749 as good measure, three-bayed with very large arches and pediment. Contrasting with this is their Victorian extension adjoining, six more bays and arches of 1810. So to St John's Street which runs along west of the Minster, appropriately low-roofed and quiet.

It was near here that John of Beverley built a church and founded a monastery at the end of the seventh century. Born at Harpham near Great Driffield he was later trained by Abbess Hilda at Whitby, and in 687 became bishop of Hexham, in 705 bishop of York. He retired to his monastery during the last three years of his life, and was buried in the church he founded. Details of his busy life come down to us from the great Bede himself, who was one of John's pupils. In the ninth century the monastery was destroyed by the Danes; in the tenth century it was refounded by King Athelstan as a collegiate church with the rights of sanctuary which it retained until the Reformation. John had been canonised in 1037, his remains enshrined, and Beverley became a place of pilgrimage. Henry V visited it to give thanks for his Agincourt victory. At the end of the reign of Henry VIII the college was dissolved, and Queen Elizabeth made the Minster a parish church, which it is today. But what a church!

Without any collegiate buildings, and with a large field to its south, Beverley Minster stands in splendid isolation, a glory in gleaming white stone. Bigger than many of our cathedrals, it is the culmination of 250 years of building, recognised as being one of the great churches of the western world. Building started at the east end around 1230 and soon reached the main transepts, so that the whole of the Lady Chapel, the great transepts and the lesser ones to the east, and the lovely choir itself show the perfect purity of the Early English lancet windows and soaring lines to the pointed arches. The east window is a fifteenth-century addition.

Most of the nave is fourteenth-century, about 1330–60, and the incomparable west front was completed by about 1450, its twin towers rising to their embattled and pinnacled crowns 200 feet above the ground. The slender grace and marvellously grouped vertical lines emphasise that this really is the Perpendicular style, so that as you view the Minster as a whole its different building styles are easily identified, yet the total effect is one of remarkable harmony.

Space forbids a catalogue of its architectural delights and details. They should be savoured slowly, from the sumptuously canopied and panelled north porch, by way of the Percy tomb – commemorating we know not whom – and what Pevsner regards as the finest funerary monument in Britain in the Decorated style, to the austerely plain and simple stone seat, the Frid Stool, surviving from the Anglo-Saxon collegiate church of King Athelstan, the centrepiece of its rights of sanctuary, giving to fugitives who sat in it 30 days of grace while the canons tried to make peace between the criminal and his pursuers. Contrasting with its simple sanctity is the woodwork of the choir, the stalls of 1520 having possibly the finest set of misericords in England, a collection of 68 whimsicalities almost all of them having two or three figures, the product of the cartoonist humour and exquisite craftsmanship of their medieval woodcarvers.

Beverley is a town to be wandered through slowly, preferably in the company of Ivan and Elisabeth Hall, whose beautiful book, *Historic Beverley*, was sponsored by Beverley Corporation to commemorate the four hundredth anniversary of Queen Elizabeth granting the charter of incorporation in 1573. Photographs, drawings and text present a comprehensive picture of this finest of East Riding towns. The Halls themselves live in a beautiful Georgian house in Hengate, but are the first to recognise that there is still much property in the town that is distinctly run-down and for which urgent restoration should be a priority. Beckside, at the south-east corner by Beverley Beck, is one example. Manifestly, much has been done in the town. Almshouses, industrial buildings, and the very early gasworks – these survive to emphasise the fact that Beverley is not just a museum in which to live, but a place of work and trade. Equally, on race days, it is a place of leisure, and at summer weekends too the pastures up at Westwood are thronged with both locals and visitors taking advantage of the ancient rights of common movement over the open fields. The early benefactors would, I hope, delight in this.

The main road A.164 from Beverley to Great Driffield touches a number of villages, some of them worth a little diversion, others better passed by quickly. Leconfield, the first of these after leaving Beverley's northern extension of Molescroft, has little to commend it today. To the south-west of the road a large moat surrounds the few green humps which remain of one of the great fortified homes of the Percys that stood here from the fifteenth century until the seventeenth century, by which time it had become a ruin. In more recent times the Royal Air Force has been associated with the village, their Leconfield station being opened in December, 1936. Fighter Command based its 249 Squadron there in 1940, but Leconfield is now one of the main R.A.F. engineering bases.

Farther on, Scorborough has one of Pearson's estate-type churches built by the Hothams of Dalton Hall, and having, like the South Dalton church, a slender spire soaring above the trees. Beswick, two miles north, is bypassed by the main road, but one house, Beswick Hall, justifies a digression. Started in 1590 it shows a simple brick classical front, looking down the lawn and the drive to the village street, restrained and dignified, an excellent example of the small country house in a village.

Two more worthwhile villages about a mile west of the main road are reached by parallel lanes. Lockington is the southerly one, a dispersed collection of pleasant little houses, tall beeches and elms, a roadside stream, and a lovely little church hiding away at the end of a lane. Its small brick tower rises from the gabled west end of the low nave, and the Norman south door has an unusual niche cut into its western side. Undoubtedly the most arresting feature is the Estoft Chapel, which was panelled in 1634, and decorated throughout with innumerable rows of heraldic achievements associated with the family, 173 shields altogether. In the centre of all this emblazonment Mary Moyser, 1633, lies uncomfortably stiff on her side, one hand holding a book, the other resting on a skull.

Kilnwick is just over a mile to the north. The Grimstons lived here; their house has gone but its huge, square, brick-enclosed eighteenth-century kitchen garden remains with its handsome little pavilion. Along the road at the southern end of the village, and near to some good modern Georgian-type houses, Townend Farm has its three front windows recessed in huge brick arches, an unusual whimsy of the mid-eighteenth century, and bearing a distinct resemblance to both Ann Routh's Hospital and Tymperon's Hospital at Beverley.

The next village, Watton, justifies a diversion eastwards to see the church and the remains of the priory. From the roadside the church appears to be roofless, the result of it having parapets above the nave and chancel, and nothing else. The broad tower is similarly squat, so that the whole structure is strangely blunt. It dates from the late fifteenth and sixteenth centuries.

A few grassy mounds in a field beyond the trees north of the church mark the site of Watton Priory, founded by Eustace Fitzjohn in 1150 for the Gilbertine order which had originated only ten years earlier with Gilbert of Sempringham, in Lincolnshire. Gilbertine houses were for nuns, but were served by resident canons, so the priory had to consist of two separate lay-outs. The ground plan at Watton was fully traced last century, showing it to be the largest foundation of the Gilbertine order, although at the Dissolution in 1539 the community consisted of two prioresses and 12 nuns, a prior and seven canons.

The double house extended for about 600 feet, the nuns having the western part, the canons the eastern one. They shared the church but, so that they could not see each other there was a wall down the nave and presbytery, the nuns using the north side of it, the canons the south. Cloisters to the north of the church were separated by a cemetery and a high wall, with a communicating passage linking them having a revolving hatch in it through which things could be passed.

All that survives of Watton Priory is the Prior's House which has been incorporated with the private house east of the present church. The fifteenth-century Prior's Hall forms the western range of the present house, a rectangular building of brick, with angle turrets and a beautiful five-sided oriel of two storeys with stone panelling between them. Each of the three storeys of the main building is a complete hall in itself, and the whole arrangement is made more atractive with stone window mouldings, contrasting with the mellowed brickwork.

Two miles north of Watton is Hutton Cranswick, two villages with one church. Cranswick is the more southerly village, with a huge and impressive methodist church just off the main road, while farther down the street is the delightful little railway station by G. T. Andrews at his 1843 simplest, having an elegant shed (now a workshop) with round arches, and a small classical house. Even better, it is still used regularly by the trains from Hull to Bridlington. Between station and methodist church, and central in the village, is a very large green with an ugly modern concrete pond. The small triangular green adjoining the church at Hutton, is an altogether more satisfying place. At the time of the eighteenth-century enclosures on the eastern margins of the Wolds where local timber was scarce, many posts and palings for fences were imported at Hull and shipped up the River Hull to Corps Landing, at the eastern end of Hutton Cranswick parish, and then carried by wagons to the various Wold landowners.

West from Hutton a lane leads across to Kirkburn. Alternatively, we can continue along the A.164 to the outskirts of Great Driffield, and then turn left along the A.163, the main Pocklington road, which brings us to Kirkburn in a couple of miles. There is little of note in the village; the church has all the glory, being second only to North Newbald in Norman workmanship in the East Riding. Nave, chancel arch, north and south doorways, many windows, and the crudely-carved font are all good Norman work, as is part of the tower, although its top stage is Perpendicular. Pearson rebuilt the chancel for Sir Tatton Sykes in 1856–7, but for me the most unusual feature of the building is the extraordinary staircase to the tower. Stone steps slant up two of the inner faces of the tower open to the nave, and then continue spirally within the thickness of the wall.

Continuing south-west along the A.163, Bainton is the next village lying partly on the main road, partly to the east of it. The large fourteenth-century church occupies a commanding site on a green mound, and the building itself is impressively unified. A splendid assembly of gargoyles and grotesques look down in their fanciful stony silences and inside, the high arcades, supported on fine octagonal piers, contribute an impression of spacious dignity.

Three miles southwards, and also to the east of the B.1248 is Lund, whose size indicates a greater importance in the past than it has now. On a small green in the middle of the village stands the old market cross on its plinth of very worn stone steps, and nearby is the little forge, pantile-roofed and with its venerable wooden door heavily embedded with blacksmith's nails. A group of sycamores on the green are known as the 'Cockpit Trees' since they mark the site of a former cockpit. The church to the north of the green is mostly a mid-nineteenth-century rebuilding but retaining its Perpendicular tower.

Suitably placed for thirsting smiths and their customers is the Wellington Inn, the proud possessor of two different inn-signs, the hanging one showing a very much younger Duke than its fellow on the front wall. A triangular green seems an informally friendly arrangement for the heart of a village, the inward-facing rows of eighteenth- and nineteenth-century houses being close enough to be neighbours, as it were, sharing the sycamores and the memory of market days. To the north a lane leads out of Lund past the church, with more good cottages, and to the east is the seventeenth-century gateway to Manor Farm.

From Lund the B.1248 continues southwards to Beverley, passing South Dalton, Etton and Cherry Burton which we have already visited. Alternatively, by heading east through Lockington the main A.164 is only three miles from Lund and Beverley can be regained along the route by which we set out.

Hull. *Top: left* (28)   Holy Trinity Church from the south-east; *right* (29)   City Hall, Queen Victoria Square, 1903–09. *Bottom* (30)   Trinity House, 1753–54.

CHAPTER TEN

The Derwent Valley

The Derwent is one of England's more unusual rivers. Rising in the moorlands of North Yorkshire about six miles from the sea, it has to flow 60 miles before it finally loses it waters and identity to the Humber. It drains 775 square miles of land, much of this in the East Riding, yet gives rise to only one town along its banks, Malton, most of which is on the North Riding side of the river. It is possible to explore its course in two parts, from York, using Stamford Bridge as the hinge on which the journeys would turn. I find it more rewarding to follow rivers downstream.

By starting at Filey and taking the A.1039 westwards until it joins the A.64, and then keeping on this to Malton, the Derwent is always to the north while the main road passes a succession of villages at the foot of the Wolds. Near Filey the River Hertford flows north and then west to join the Derwent near Ganton. The low-lying land through which both rivers flow is called The Carrs – lands liable to seasonal flooding, but improved drainage has now reduced this danger; the name survives as evidence of common grazing lands, each parish along the foot of the Wolds having its own Carrs on the map today, Folkton, Flixton, Willerby, Sherburn and Heslerton.

Each village lies just off the busy road, with minor roads leading from it, northwards to the river, southwards on to the Wolds, soon reaching 500 feet. From Folkton Brow and Staxton Brow there are magnificent views across The Carrs to the Yorkshire coast, and it is not difficult to picture the whole of the vale

31. South Dalton church: J. L. Pearson's splendid steeple, 1858–61, soars 200 feet above the surrounding landscape.

covered by Lake Pickering, 25 miles long and up to eight miles wide, an ice-barrier damming it north of Sherburn.

Ganton village lies adjacent to the beautiful parkland of Ganton Hall, the house in its Victorian French chateau style looking better through the trees than in the closer view. Some of the stone cottages in the village are single-storeyed and white-washed, a style characteristic of coastal villages of Northumbria, and here looking especially good in their sheltered setting.

Sherburn is a pleasant street village to the north of the A.64, boasting two inns, a church with a Norman tower and good sculpture inside, and an old cross dedicated, like the church, to St Hilda. A stream rises at the foot of the Wold escarpment, and has been dammed in its valley to form a mill-pond. At High Mill Farm, which has an 1843 date-stone, part of an old watermill retains some of its machinery. The mill was reconstructed in 1842 and now uses electric power to make its own animal foodstuffs.

The route of the proposed Wolds Way, the long-distance footpath from Filey to the Humber, is not here definitive, but is proposed to follow the edge of the escarpment along Heslerton Brow, taking it away from the throaty roars of the A.64's busy traffic.

At West Heslerton the church stands at the top of the village and was built by Street for Sir Tatton Sykes in 1877. Its broach spire includes four statues from the architect's work on Bristol Cathedral, and the interior is very much in the Early English style. On the south wall is an enormous marble monument to Sir Christopher Sykes, who died of a consumption at Clifton, near Bristol, on 17th September 1801, aged 52. The monument was erected by his daughter, Decima Hester Beatrix Foulis, during the Napoleonic Wars and extols her father's endeavours 'to beautify, not to deface, the features of Nature. To provide food for Man's sustenance rather than to sacrifice human life upon the shrine of victory and ambition'. Clearly, Decima thought the French Emperor made very poor comparison with her father.

A minor road from West Heslerton leads northwards across

The Carrs to Yedingham where the old stone bridge across the Derwent has been replaced by an ugly new one, but the willows by the winding, rather muddy river have their own compensating grace. A group of rather dilapidated farm buildings look across the approach road of the old bridge to the twin bell-cotes of the restored church, dwarfed by an enormous beech. From two miles above Yedingham down to Stamford Bridge the Derwent forms the boundary between North and East Ridings.

The B.1258 takes us back to the main road, which we can cross in order to visit Wintringham, a delightful village of low, chalk-fronted houses along the road which leads to the edge of the roughly-grazed pastures and mature trees of Place Newton, a brick-fronted house of 1837. The village church, one of the biggest in the district, is of Tadcaster limestone and far more interesting than a first glance might suggest. Great flat buttresses support the strongly-battlemented tower, and inside there is a fine array of Jacobean woodwork giving character to the spaciousness – pews with paired acorn-heads, a two-decker pulpit, a reader's desk, medieval screens to the aisle chapels and old stalls with some modern misericords. The tracery of the aisle windows shows a series of saints' portraits with inscriptions fifteenth- or sixteenth-century, shown on white glass stained yellow, which is apparently very rare outside York. An unusual memorial (to John Lister, 1651) takes the form of a board bearing beneath a coat-of-arms a rhyming acrostic, and on the inside wall of the tower, is an instruction to the bellringers:

> 'I pray you Gentlemen beware
> And when you ring ye Bells take care;
> For he that Rings and breaks a stay,
> Must pay Sixpence without delay.
> And if you ring in Spurs or Hatt
> You must likewise pay Sixpence for that.
> > Michael Gill, Clerk, 1723.'

Whereas Place Newton has its informal, rough-grazed park, that of Scampston Hall shows the carefully landscaped informality of Capability Brown's design of 1773 which included a neat Palladian bridge across the stream. Much of the house is Leverton's plan of 1803 for William Thomas St Quintin, its centrepiece on the great south front comprising huge Doric pilasters and a dome, with the west front having Tuscan columns. In front of the house the stream has been widened into a lake whose lower end is spanned by a handsome stone bridge of 1775, carrying the main A.64 and widened about 30 years ago.

Rillington, the next main road village, has little to commend it, but Scagglethorpe, just round the foot of Thorpe Bassett Wold, offers the reward of some nicely-grouped early nineteenth-century cottages just off the road, a foretaste of even better things to come at Settrington.

A little stream rising on the Wolds to the east of the village makes a big southward loop before trickling gently north to Settrington, through the parkland and lake of the late eighteenth-century Settrington House. This was designed by Francis Johnson about 1790 and is of stone, but was partly damaged by fire in 1963. Fronted by a beautiful lawn, with elms, yews and copper beeches around, it stands close neighbour to the church, tucked away almost at the south-east corner of the village.

Settrington Beck flows past a mill of about 1790, before dividing the two sides of this very attractive village, planned obviously as an estate village around 1800. Most of the stone cottages are paired, with two windows and doorway below, two more windows above, and stand well back from the stream. Two bridges and a ford provide focal points in a village scene which cannot have changed very much since it was rebuilt.

Three miles west of Settrington the twin towns of Malton and Norton are separated by the Derwent, crossed by a two-arched stone bridge, widened and repaired innumerable times since the first fourteenth-century structure linked the two Ridings. Norton has its best buildings in Langton Road, where a terrace of three-storey Georgian houses is a reminder of what much of the place might have been like. Hodgson Fowler's church was completed by the addition of its large impressive tower of 1913, and the keys of St Peter are carved on the stone pillars of the churchyard gates.

The minor road which leaves the A.64 in Norton at the corner by the railway follows the course of a Roman road southwards through some pleasantly undulating countryside. In three miles a side road leads to Langton, a gem not to be missed.

Langton has all the character and appearance of a village in the other parts of the Jurassic stone belt which extends south-westwards across England. Graced by a green with mature chestnuts and sycamores, flowering cherries add their colour in spring, and a well-placed seat with a plaque records that Langton won the Best Kept Village contest in the East Riding in 1973. Many of the houses are in pairs, with wide pointed 'Gothic' windows and doorways of around 1830. A terrace of four at the east end of the village has cobbles in front, with another house at right-angles looking down the green. Ivy covers many of the house fronts, in one case almost obscuring the surviving yellow disc of the old A.A. name-plate. The hall stands rather aloof in its parkland at the east end of the village, stone greyhounds at its gates. The Norcliffes lived here for many centuries; Colonel Norcliffe built the school in 1841, and, one suspects, much of the village, and, like most of the family, is commemorated in the village church which was rebuilt in 1822.

Retracing our steps westwards we aim for the best section of the whole course of the Derwent where the river has forced its way through the gorge at Kirkham, one of the classically geological landscape features of the East Riding. As though to add spiritual emphasis to the work of natural science, the valley here was chosen as the site of Kirkham Priory, now the only important monastic ruin in the East Riding.

Compared with other Yorkshire monasteries the above-ground remains at Kirkham are meagre, but the parts which do survive are architecturally fine, in a most beautiful setting, enclosed within a westward-curving sweep of the Derwent between wooded hillsides. Founded by Walter l'Espée around 1125 for Augustinian Canons, the Priory was added to, changed and developed, particularly in the thirteenth century. Fragments speak of past glories: a Norman doorway into the refectory framing a view of the valley, part of the prior's house and infirmary, and in the west wall of the cloister a beautiful lavatorium of two bays containing some exquisite tracery and mouldings. The best remains of all are seen both first and last. Apparently springing from the very earth itself the wide arch of the gatehouse leads the eye upwards to a thirteenth-century façade richly decorated and sculptured, and showing the arms of the many great families who gave patronage to the priory.

Below the priory the road winds down the hill to cross the river by Kirkham Bridge, three-arched and probably designed by Carr in 1806, but using some of the masonry of an older bridge on the site. Cutwaters continue upwards into pedestrian refuges from which you can look at the river's course downstream to a broad weir. The riverside path gives a splendid view of the priory, but Kirkham Hall on the hillside above it has its façade hidden by a group of mature copper beeches.

To stay in our province we must retrace our route up the eastern side of the valley to Westow, where the early eighteenth-century Westow Hall is prominent and the Manor House is a farm. In the lonely church a mile away a small ancient stone portrays a simple Crucifixion, while on its reverse is a cresset containing twelve shallow cups for oil lights. As the stone now forms part of a memorial this rare feature is unfortunately no longer visible.

Good things continue to abound in this part of the Derwent Valley. Near the crossroads a mile south of Westow is Gally Gap Farm, a splendid group of pantiled farm buildings in the mellowed stone of late Georgian days – elegant, prosperous, yet functional, with neat gardens, tidy fields and hedges, and mature trees. The minor road westwards past the farm leads to Howsham, a small village on the hill descending to Howsham Hall. The cottages of brown stone emphasise the fact that we are here back on the band of Jurassic rocks, for the character and colour is so markedly different from the great majority of East Riding villages.

The cottages at Howsham are only along the east side of the

single street, facing trees on the opposite side bordering How-sham Park. Up to about 1770 the village extended down both sides of a wide green, but Nathaniel Cholmley made great changes to his parklands which necessitated the removal of part of the village and the replacement of a number of cottages by trees. The effect was to produce a strangely lop-sided village, which is nevertheless very attractive.

Howsham Hall is now a school. Its south front of stone, two-storeyed, and consistently Jacobean (1619), has its central doorway between paired Doric columns with paired Corinthian ones above. The original house had two wings to the north, but the remodelling of the 1770s which changed the interior layout included changes to the wings. By the drive which curves round to the hall is the stable-block, also of *c.* 1775, and having a prominent cupola above its western entrance.

George Hudson, the 'Railway King', was born at Howsham in 1800, and after his death in London in 1871 was buried at Scrayingham, the next village down the Derwent, whose course below the four-arched bridge at Howsham follows as many twists and turns as did Hudson's life. Some of his forebears are commemorated by a sloping stone slab to the south of the church tower, and George Hudson's name is one of a number of members of his family recorded on a nearby marble.

By now the Derwent has become a mature meandering river in its broadening vale, and three miles below Scrayingham is crossed by Stamford Bridge, which now carries the main A.166 York–Great Driffield road. Traffic lights control the flow across the narrow but graceful three-arched bridge of 1727 which replaced an earlier one of timber, probably on stone piers. The peaceful riverside meadows nearby were the site of the last Saxon victory on English soil, when, in 1066, King Harold fought his brother Tostig and Harald Hardrada of Norway whose warriors prepared for an assault on York. King Harold and his Saxon army had been guarding the Kent coast, but when he heard of the Norse invasion he took his troops northwards in one of the most spectacular marches in our military history. For most of a September day the armies were locked in savage combat involving 100,000 men in which the enemy was beaten, its leaders slain, but it was not long before Harold, after victory celebrations at York, had to take his tired troops south to subsequent defeat at Hastings.

Some of the spoils of battle are occasionally dug up from the fields and the river, and it is quite probable that much more is still buried beneath the quiet turf. A simple stone on a grassy bank by the main road through Stamford Bridge records, in English and Norwegian, the bare outline of the event. Nearby the North Wolds District Council has created an attractive garden of sloping lawns, shrubs, and flowers, with a splendid view of the handsome, six-storeyed brick watermill, now enjoying a new lease of life as a popular restaurant. The mill-race flows beneath it, curving round to meet the parent river below the weir. A riverside path gives access to its banks where fishermen ply their skills, and the Derwent up to here is navigable by small pleasure craft. Below Stamford Bridge the river loses its dual allegiance and for the rest of its winding way to the Ouse it belongs wholly to the East Riding, the A.166 taking over its boundary function as far as York and the Ouse.

Minor roads through the twin small villages of High and Low Catton lead to the main A.1079, Beverley road which crosses the river by a modern bridge at Kexby. Happily, the oldest bridge across the Derwent survives as a near neighbour, no longer used by traffic. Kexby Bridge has three arches and has 1650 inscribed on the parapet. Elvington Bridge, another three miles down the Derwent, is of similar structure though 50 years later.

By now we have joined the B.1228 York–Howden road, passing through Elvington and Sutton-upon-Derwent on opposite banks of the river. Elvington has a pleasant grouping of houses round a small green, Sutton a large, gaunt, derelict watermill, with the church occupying a commanding situation nearby on a high mound above the river.

For the moment we shall keep to the west of the river and follow the network of lanes steadily southwards to the Ouse returning to York for a more westerly route which will enable us to see some of the villages in this south-east corner of the Riding. Wheldrake is worth taking the trouble to find, for it is a good street village of a variety of houses, including a half-timbered one and several very attractive stone cottages. Modern development to the north is eating into good farmland but not spoiling the village façade. Eastwards from the village, past the church, the lane soon turns sharply to pass the parklands of Thicket Priory. Fragments of a Benedictine priory exist here, but the building visible from the road is early Victorian Tudor, now used as a Carmelite monastery.

The winter-flooded meadows of the Derwent here are called Wheldrake Ings, 400 acres of low-lying land recently acquired by the Yorkshire Naturalists' Trust as a Reserve for the winter home of thousands of waterfowl including Bewick's and whooper swans, widgeon, teal, pochard and other species of ducks.

Thorganby village was a Norse settlement and now at its southern end has a small Georgian house, Thorganby Hall, with the brick church opposite, and a good farm group nearby including a dovecote and a horse-gin retaining its original timber structure inside. South-west of Thorganby the glacial deposits of the Vale contain sandy top-soils resulting in a heathy landscape where birches and Scots pines predominate to give a welcome change in the scenery of the East Riding. Such an area is Skipwith Common extending over 850 acres, and since 1954, a Site of Special Scientific Interest, of which 600 acres are leased to the Yorkshire Naturalists' Trust.

Accessible by footpaths and bridleways from the A.163 on the south and the minor road between Skipwith and Cliffe on the east, the common contains both dry and wet heaths, with a number of pools. Consequently, plant, insect and bird life is very varied, 90 regular breeding species of birds being recorded, including all three woodpeckers and five of the owls. A colony of black-headed gulls breeds on the pools which also house a wintering population of wildfowl. As there is plenty of car-parking space near the main southern entrance, Skipwith Common is a popular spot for visitors interested in the wild life, and a Nature Trail helps them to identify many of the species inhabiting this lowland area of almost primeval landscape character.

At Skipwith roads meet at a large triangular green with a pond, the village extending westwards along a no-through road. Timbered cottages are a reminder of the woodlands which once characterised this part of the East Riding, while the splendid church has its roots in Saxon days. The lovely mottled stonework of the two lower stages of its tower is Anglo-Saxon, with the bell stage added 400 years later. There is a Saxon arch to the nave, and the south door shows a masterpiece of decorative ironwork which looks thirteenth-century, but is apparently nineteenth-century work. Whatever its date, the artistry is superb.

Five miles away to the south, and now bypassed by the A.163, Hemingborough was always the largest village between the Derwent and the Ouse, and in 1743 when the parish included some of the surrounding smaller villages, its population of over 1,200 was larger than those of Pocklington or Market Weighton. Its population fell during the next 100 years, while those of the market towns nearer the Wolds increased. Not only was there movement locally but a number of people emigrated overseas. Many parishes having by the 1800s most of the fields enclosed, cultivation was at a maximum, but in the small market towns factories and mills had been built and were attracting the labour from the countryside.

The streets of Hemingborough form a square, and contain a number of good eighteenth-century houses and farms, particularly in the main street which runs southwards to the church. Originally under the prior and monks of Durham, the church became collegiate in 1426 by when most of the present beautiful building was completed. Inside it has the most complete set of bench-ends in the East Riding, showing figures of two-headed dragons, a monkey, a jester, a courtier, and some nondescript animals. In the stalls is one misericord only, but this is probably the oldest in England, dating from *c*. 1200.

Westwards along the A.63, the main road goes first to Barlby where we join the A.19 for York. At Riccall is the third really fine church in this leg of our tour between Derwent and Ouse.

Basically Norman, with an elaborate south doorway of three orders, the arcades were added in the thirteenth century, the south chapel is Perpendicular, and the whole building gleams in its Tadcaster stone. Although the main A.19 continues northwards to Escrick, passing extensive woodlands on the east, we shall detour to the west, keeping watch on the Ouse, from which, at Wheel Hall a mile from Riccall, Harald Hardrada's huge army landed in 1066. Beyond Kelfield we join the B.1222 which has crossed the Ouse at Cawood by the first bridge below York, and soon find ourselves at Stillingfleet, the main purpose of this diversion.

Once again it is the church which calls our attention. As at Skipwith, the whole range of medieval styles of building is represented, pride of place going to the exceptionally detailed Norman south doorway with its five orders, and the great wooden door itself, whose ironwork is distinctly Viking, especially in the representation of a small ship and figures in the top left-hand corner. In the churchyard a small yew casts its dark shade over an unusual memorial, to ten carol singers and the parish clerk, buried in a communal grave, after being accidentally drowned in the River Ouse whilst returning from singing the praises of their Saviour in the neighbouring townships on 26 December 1833. There are other good memorials in the churchyard which overlooks a broad sweep of rough village pasture gently sloping to an insignificant-looking stream. However, a plaque on the stone bridge commemorates the 'Great Flood of March 22–29, 1947', when the depth of water reached 21 feet.

Some of the village is on a ridge of higher ground to the south, and a minor road follows this eastwards to Escrick, joining the main A.19 opposite Escrick Park. This was once the home of Sir Thomas Knyvet whose chief claim to fame was his discovery of the gunpowder barrels in the cellars of the Houses of Parliament in 1605. The present house was originally built around 1690, but was refronted and heightened in 1758, with wings and stables added five years later to John Carr's designs. Escrick Hall is now a girls' boarding school, with a fine playing field in its beautiful park, rich with mature oaks and chestnuts, while the rhododendrons add their colours to Holly Carr

Woods to the south. There is some neat nineteenth-century estate housing near the entrance gates to the hall, and in the village, at commuter distance from York, good modern houses of traditional design have little bridges giving access over a small stream.

Naburn, on the B.1222, is equidistant from Stillingfleet and Escrick, the village lying between the road and the river, which here swings round in a wide loop. The old blacksmith's shop has been converted into the headquarters of the Yorkshire Ouse Sailing Club, formed in 1938 by Commander Palmer of Naburn Hall. A jetty extends along the front lawn of the club house, adjacent to the ramp from which a chain ferry operated across the river to Acaster Malbis until 1956. The twin villages are popular sailing centres, and most weekends see some racing on this stretch of the Ouse, with the Club moorings and land on the west bank more easily accessible to the many members who come from the industrial West Riding towns.

Now to look at the land between the Derwent and the Wolds, picking up our previous journey at Sutton-upon-Derwent and continuing down the B.1228 to Howden. The road soon crosses the Pocklington Canal by Hagg Bridge, and then swings through a right angle past the woodlands of Ross Moor, before we take the first of three digressions westwards towards the river. East Cottingwith has a brick church of 1780, a former Friends' Meeting House converted into a Victorian school, and an inviting path through the meadows to East Cottingwith Lock on the canal which joins the Derwent a few hundred yards away.

Two miles south is Ellerton, at the end of a lane, where Pearson's 1847 church replaced the old one which was a survivor from the thirteenth-century Gilbertine Priory. Some of the original stained glass has been re-used in the heads of the nave windows. Aughton is another 'lane-end' village, forlorn in the flood-plain of the Derwent whose waters sometimes reach the churchyard. The earthworks of the motte-and-bailey castle have over the centuries watched the rise and fall of the river which helped to fill the moat of the manor house of the Askes. It was Sir Robert Aske who led the Pilgrimage of Grace from Yorkshire in 1536, mustering over 30,000 men on Skip-with Moor in October. Early success, followed by assurances of royal pardons for participants gave some encouragement; but after subsequent misgivings on the part of the king, the uprising was put down, and Aske was finally executed at York in July 1537. A farmhouse occupies the site of their old home east of the church, whose splendid chancel arch is rich with Norman zig-zag and beakheads; and an armoured Sir Richard Aske looks coldly from his portrait brass of 1460.

Bubwith lies along the A.163 west of its crossing our B.1228, the battlemented and pinnacled church tower commanding a wooded bank above a loop in the river with a path along the meadows by the waterside. One unusual feature inside the church is a helmet and wooden sword carried at old family funerals centuries ago. The village contains some attractive late Georgian houses, and a gothicised Wesleyan chapel of 1796, enlarged in 1870, retains its numbered box pews. Beneath the three-arched stone bridge of 1793 the Derwent flows sluggishly southwards paralleled by a minor road through Breighton to Wressle and the A.63.

Wressle retains the only important castle in the East Riding, built about 1380 for Sir Thomas Percy. Its two surviving massive towers hold the south range between them, containing the hall. The west tower was of three storeys, the east one of four, and included the chapel; stair turrets project above the towers, and from the tops of these it is said you can see 30 churches. Ogee-headed windows adorn the hall range, but most of the other have two lights and transoms, the whole effect suggesting a trend towards the comforts of a manor house and away from the harsher necessities of fortification. Much of the castle was demolished at the end of the Civil War, a serious fire in 1796 almost completing the process. A quarter of a mile south over the railway (Selby–Hull line), Wressle's church is relatively modern. Dating from 1799 it is wholly of brick, coursed in Yorkshire bond, which differs from English and Flemish bond in having one row of headers to every three rows of stretchers.

Howden is the largest town in this southern sector of the East Riding, between Hull and Selby. It should be so much better than it is, for within its rather intricate street-pattern there are many houses of the last 200 years which are distinctly seedy. Howden was an important market town with one of the most noble of English parish churches, whose magnificent tower dominates the surrounding countryside. Although the church became collegiate in 1267, most of the present building is late thirteenth- and early fourteenth-century. The original chancel collapsed in 1696, and the octagonal chapter-house, now a ruin, in 1750. Bishop Skirlaw of Durham had built it at the end of the fourteenth century about the same time as he started the crossing tower.

From almost any angle Howden's parish church looks magnificent, a small cathedral. From the Market Square its tower is seen framed in the ruined east window; from the south its greatness contrasts with the ruined chapter-house. Inside the story of the church is told pictorially in a display of appliqué work in the south transept, detailed, colourful, and very human. Nearby is an extract from Bentley's *Quarterly Review* of 1859 recording Dickens' description of Howden Horse Fair. There is also a pauper's coffin and a horse-plough known as an Oliver digger made in the 1920s. Much of the woodwork in the church is modern, the great south door, the choir stalls, altar, and the south transept furnishings all show the familiar church mouse symbol of Robert Thompson's workshops at Kilburn.

A minor road west from Howden leads to Barmby-on-the-Marsh near the end of the Derwent's course. On the way it passes Knedlington Old Hall, a handsome brick house of the early seventeenth century, and at Barmby brick was used in the church's eighteenth-century tower and in the National School of 1834 next to the churchyard. Beyond the end of the village the Derwent meets the Ouse.

Boats could once sail up the Derwent as far as Yedingham Bridge, but large barges could only reach Malton, 38 miles upstream. Now, the navigation is limited to the 15 miles as far as the tidal lock at Sutton-on-Derwent, site of the first lock on the original navigation of about 1720. By the end of the eighteenth century other locks had been built at Stamford Bridge, Buttercrambe, Howsham, and Kirkham, together with lock-keepers' brick cottages. Where the Derwent meets the Ouse there was a chain-keeper's cottage and a jetty.

The Derwent contributed to its own decline as a navigation, for much of the sand and gravel used in building the York and Scarborough Railway was transported along the river. From 1845 the river's story followed the usual pattern of the canals – take-over by the railway, subsequent neglect, and a lingering death, although navigation to Cottingwith lasted until 1930. However, the Yorkshire Derwent Trust has the laudable aim of restoring the navigation to Malton again, opening up the river as a leisure waterway so that the beauties of Stamford Bridge, Howsham and Kirkham, may be accessible by water. In 1972 the first hurdle was passed in the rebuilding of the lock at Sutton, making navigation now possible to Stamford Bridge.

The A.614 is a fast, direct route north-east from Howden to Holme-upon-Spalding-Moor, seven featureless miles away. Rarely exceeding 20 feet above sea-level this part of the Vale contained the largest common pastures in the East Riding, which remained badly drained and unenclosed until the late eighteenth century. Few shelter-belts break the skyline, so that the 150 foot Church Hill at Holme-upon-Spalding- Moor takes on a greater landscape importance. South of Holme, Work-house Farm is by the main road, and was built in 1790 as a workhouse for both sexes. Of its two original lock-ups, the west one, for women, survives, but only just. Beyond, a sign-post has achieved a little fame as pointing down a lane to 'Land of Nod', a farm two miles away by the Market Weighton Canal.

Holme village extends a mile along both sides of the A.163, west of its junction with our A.614, while its church crowns the hill to the east. Happily escaping the Victorian restorers it retains its early nineteenth-century box pews and much older pulpit complete with sounding board. The west tower is bat-tlemented, and from the windy churchyard is a magnificent panorama of the plain reaching to the Ouse and Humber, with the line of the Wolds on the east completing a landscape so much of which has been shaped by the hands of man. There is nothing spectacular about the wooded hill except that it is the only one for miles, a landmark, and the site of an ancient beacon which blew down in 1840.

North of Church Hill a minor road leads to Everingham, giving occasional distant views through the trees to the park of Everingham Hall, built by Carr about 1760, one time a seat of the Duke of Norfolk, and for the last few years the home of Lady Fitzalan Howard. The huge Catholic chapel of 1836 is an Italian basilica in an English park, with white stuccoed walls outside, and an interior for which spectacular is scarcely a strong enough description. Giant Corinthian columns, marble statues in niches, a gold and white tunnel-vaulted ceiling, are breathtaking in their splendour, so that outside again it is a relief to look upon the cool green reflective beauties of the long lake to the north of the hall, and the gay flower gardens of the cottages in the village.

Westwards to Seaton Ross and Bielby, unpretentious villages of brick, yet possessing some splendid sundials. Bielby's Wesleyan chapel of 1837 has a very elegant one above its doorway, while Seaton Ross claims the biggest sundial in England. On the wall of a cottage, its white painted half-circle is 12 feet across, with an enormous projecting gnomon. Another, smaller, sundial is above the church door, and William Watson, who made all these local sundials in the nineteenth century, is buried in a sunny corner of the quiet churchyard.

Crossing the Pocklington Canal by Walbut Lock we can cut north to Allerthorpe and the main Beverley road. At Barmby Moor, just off the main road, the broad open village green may be the site of a former market place, for in the seventeenth and eighteenth centuries this was a little market town which could not successfully compete with its more important neighbour, Pocklington. At one end of the green the elegant manor-house is screened by trees, and two miles west on the main road the New Inn was originally a famous coaching inn of the late eighteenth century.

North from Barmby minor roads lead to Fangfoss where mature beeches and limes shade the path to the church, restored in 1850 but largely re-using the original Norman masonry and preserving well the corbel-table and a good south doorway. Behind the church is Fangfoss Hall of mellowed

Georgian brick, and the National School of 1867 is just across the way, by a green.

Many small becks flow westwards from the spring-line at the foot of the Wolds escarpment, none significant in itself, yet each is named, and each has given justification for Saxon or Danish settlements. Sometimes the same beck has different names at the various parts of its short life, usually after it has been joined by a small feeder. At Wilberfoss willows fringe the beck, with little bridges spanning it, and of the many attractive cottages, the Post Office is especially noticeable because of its Georgian bow windows. Happily, the main road now by-passes the village, leaving it to ponder its quiet history and memories of the Wilberforce family who had left it centuries before William gave it a minor reflected glory. That same main road can take us past the old Kexby bridge the few miles back to York, but our thoughts must turn southwards for the last part of our East Riding journeyings, along the Humber shore to Hull.

CHAPTER ELEVEN

Humberwards to Hull

The proposed route of the M62 enters the East Riding south of Howden, crossing the Ouse near Boothferry Bridge. It is to be hoped that the new bridge will be more cleanly elegant than the hideous structure of 1929, which carries the A.614 from the West Riding. The M62 will merge with the A.63 east of Howden, but our present route to Hull will take us much closer to the river.

Factories and jetties front the Ouse at Howden Dyke, one mile from Howden, and a road accompanies the embankment along the sweeping convex bend of the river as far as Goole Bridge, which carries the railway across this busy stretch of the river. There the road swings inland through a right-angle, passes through the pasture parkland of Saltmarshe Hall, and then heads north for Laxton, where old and new churches stand on opposite sides of the road. Eastwards then through the fenland-type landscape almost at sea level, to rejoin the riverside embankment near Blacktoft. To see the river you have to leave the road and climb the bank. Broad, brown and muddy, the Ouse glides towards the sea.

Blacktoft Sand on the opposite side of the river is reclaimed saltings and marshland, one of the last English breeding places of the avocet in 1837 before their return to Suffolk a century later. At the eastern corner of the sands the two great rivers Trent and Ouse merge to form the Humber, a mature river half a mile wide. At Faxfleet the road leaves the riverside, cutting inland for four miles to join the A.63 west of Newport, the only East Riding village created by the industrial revolution.

Before 1780, the whole of this area was covered by Walling

Fen, 5,000 acres of ill-drained land whose carrs were used as summer pastures and whose peat was cut as fuel from the fourteenth century onwards. Difficult to drain, being at least five feet below the level of the Humber's spring tides it also had many commons, but by 1760 these were being enclosed. Between 1772 and 1782 the Market Weighton Canal was cut with the dual function of drainage channel and inland navigation linking the Humber with Market Weighton. It ended two miles short of the town, four locks and nine miles from the Humber, and during the digging of its channel extensive deposits of good-quality clay were discovered, suitable for brick and tile making. A works developed, and the village of Newport sprang into existence, along both sides of the canal for a short distance northwards from the A.63, and along both sides of the main road itself. The best part is on the east bank of the canal where a row of pleasant brick houses is separated from the water by a narrow road and grassy canal bank, not far enough away from the A.63 however, for its incessant traffic roar to be lost.

The canal is now mainly dry above Sod House lock, three miles from Newport, but acquires surface water drainage, supplemented by the in-flow of the little River Foulness, keeping the channel watered down to the Humber, which it joins at Weighton Lock. This is a sea lock, having two pairs of both sea gates and navigation gates, allowing two-way operation according to the tides. The canal is likely to continue functioning as a drain but not as a navigation.

Broomfleet is the only village east of the canal and south of the A.63, a settlement on reclaimed land, where pylons straddle the dreary landscape and power-lines savage the sky. Gaunt chimneys of brickworks by the canal to the west throw up their accusing fingers, but nature has helped to hide the scars of the old clay-pits, now willow-fringed and favoured by fishermen. Southwards, the Humber is by now almost a mile and a half broad where it sweeps round from Whitton Sand to Pudding Pie Sand opposite Brough.

From Broomfleet the road goes past Provence and Providence to Ellerker, south of the A.63 near the Caves, then joins the line of the Roman road which enters Brough by the golf-course. Brough upon Humber was an important link on the Roman road from Lincoln to York, with a ferry crossing the river by Pudding Pie Sand. The Romans called it Petuaria at the beginning of the second century when a turf rampart had been constructed round the town, later rebuilt as a stone wall nine feet thick, with rectangular towers 25 feet high, one of which has been excavated in some detail. In 1937 was discovered an inscribed stone which recorded the gift of a theatrical stage by one Marcus Ulpius Janarius, an aedilis, or tribal magistrate, an unusually high-ranking official for so small a town. This suggests that during the second century Roman Britain had self-governing cantons, based on the old tribal capitals. Since only three other towns had theatres (St Albans, Colchester and Canterbury), it looks as though there was a genuine attempt to bring to the capital of the Parisi a touch of culture from the more civilised south.

Three miles eastwards, at North Ferriby, the Wolds reach the Humber shore, re-appearing on the Lincolnshire side just over two miles away. A belt of woodland, the Long Plantation, forms an excellent shelter-belt for the western part of this large and growing village. Pearson designed the church; it is one of his earlier ones, built of small brown stones and having a broach spire. Ferriby Hall is far more impressive, for in 1760 Sir Henry Etherington, a Hull merchant, built it of brick with stone quoins, adding an obelisk three years later a few hundred yards behind the house. One unexpectedly good thing about North Ferriby is that the Parish Council has provided a carpark on the foreshore, which, with its view along the Humber, has become a popular venue for motorists.

Hessle has almost been devoured by the maw of Hull, but has just managed to retain some aspects of individuality, especially on its western fringe, and around its handsome church, whose beautiful modern baptistry was designed by a local architect. Nearby is a wide Market Square where new façades now outnumber the old. To the west of the church a few grey-brick late Georgian houses survive, and there are Victorian terraces. But Hessle's skyline and waterfront are changing, for it is here that the new Humber Bridge will step into the East Riding to form the first direct link across the river, a century after the idea had first been put forward.

In 1872 it was planned to build a railway tunnel through the chalk bed of the river between Hessle and Barton, but the idea was dropped, to be re-awakened early this century, but with no positive outcome. A scheme for a multi-span bridge was promoted in 1931, but a financial crisis put that idea out of court for another generation. Then, in 1969, the Humber Bridge Board was given permission to press ahead with plans for a huge single-span suspension-type road bridge to be built, work commencing in 1972, and completion expected in 1976. With a central span of 4,626 feet – much greater than similar bridges across the Severn and Forth estuaries – it will be the largest bridge of its type anywhere in the world. Linked to the further eastwards extension of the M62 it will make an enormous difference to all traffic movements in eastern England, and hence to the economy and commerce of the new region of Humberside. Of all bridges, those of the suspension type are the most graceful in their flowing lines; artists' drawings of the Humber Bridge suggest that we shall certainly be made to lift our eyes skywards from the Humber's swift but turgid waters.

Hull is the short name for this city of nearly 300,000 people, which is now England's third port. It started as a tiny trading settlement called Wyke, where the River Hull joined the Humber. Edward I obtained it from Meaux Abbey in 1293, renaming it Kingston-upon-Hull and granting it a municipal charter in 1299.

In 1331 it was allowed to elect a mayor, the first one being a great merchant, Sir William de la Pole. By 1321 permission was granted to fortify the town by a moat and later a wall of brick, enclosing a gridiron layout of streets like that of Winchelsea. The line of the former docks replaced the original medieval moat, effectively islanding the Old Town between them, the River Hull, and the Humber waterfront.

Queen Victoria Square is the hub around which so much of Hull's life today throbbingly revolves. It stands on the line of the old moat and the old docks. Southwards, behind the

Ferens Art Gallery, is Princess Dock, built about 1827; beyond it is Rennie's Humber Dock of 20 years earlier, with an arm leading to Railway Dock of 1846. All are closed, but retain locks and bridges, with gigantic warehouses of about 1850, stark against the skyline, dark, derelict, and broken-windowed. The docks have water but their life has gone.

North-east of Queen Victoria Square is the great oasis of Queen's Gardens, carrying the eye eastwards to the modern buildings of the College of Technology and the Police Head-quarters. Queen's Dock used to be here, built between 1774 and 1778, the first one outside London, and the nascent point of the growth of the modern port of Hull. But in 1930 when it was filled in, conservation was not a word in the planning vocabulary. So Hull lost a unique asset, a dock which brought vessels to the city's heart. It gained a flower garden – a good one, let it be said, with ponds and shrubs and quiet corners. But a vitality has been lost here as it also has in Old Town, which lies south and east of the Gardens.

The tall, blackened monument to William Wilberforce sepa-rates the gardens from the college, and Lowgate leads south-wards past the end of the Guildhall, across Alfred Gelder Street, where Lowgate soon becomes Market Place. St Mary's Church opposite has the lower part of its seventeenth-century tower pierced so that the street pavement passes through it – part of Scott's 1861 restoration of the medieval church. In this part of Lowgate are some good Victorian commercial buildings.

Further down Market Place is Holy Trinity, the largest English parish church, and the first major building to use brick in its construction. Transepts and chancel, dating from 1300–1360, show this early masonry of red and blue bricks, now age-mellowed. The nave is later, and the crossing tower of 1500 still dominates Old Town, for the newer concrete monoliths of the city are much further to the west. Clerestory windows make the interior really light, its great length emphasised by the slender pillars and the height of the colour-ful roof, the beauty of its details and furnishings deserving the fullest appraisal.

Immediately to the north of the church is the covered market, while the beautiful west front looks down on the awnings of the stalls permanently sited in the open-air market. On Tuesdays, Fridays and Saturdays trade takes precedence and the market's lively hours are followed by the legacy of litter. Nearby is Trinity House, dating from 1753 but starting as a religious body in 1368, making it an older foundation than either London or Newcastle. By the mid-sixteenth century it had become a guild of mariners, and Elizabeth granted a second charter additional to that of Humber pilotage and the care of buoys and lights in the river. These original duties are no longer carried on, but the foundation maintains a number of sailors' almshouses and, in 1787, started to train seamen for the Royal and Merchant Navies, and the Pilot Service, work which has been continued ever since.

On the south side of the market stalls a high building of dark bricks was the Grammar School from 1583–1878; there also met the Society of Merchant Venturers until 1706. Now it is a warehouse. From Old Town, so much of the historic soul of Hull has taken flight. In the Market Place Peter Sheemakers' 1734 gilt equestrian statue of William III surveys the melancholy scene.

East of Market Place is High Street, once the most important street in Hull. Many of its buildings are desolate, derelict, yet as you wander along its narrow length you do find some astonishing surprises. Maister's House was the home of a great merchant family, and after its rebuilding in 1743 was used as both a residence and a counting-house until 1833. Severe outside, its entrance hall and stairway are decorated with great elegance and delicacy. The National Trust now owns it.

Higher up, on the opposite side and looking across waste land, is Wilberforce House, an eighteenth-century remodelling of a late Tudor building. The house came into the Wilberforce family in the eighteenth century and in it William was born in 1759. Various rooms in the house are given over to the display of collections – period dolls' clothing, butterflies – but by far the most unhappily impressive is the Slave Room, with its nauseating evidence of man's inhumanity to man. It comes as a definite shock to see, in a nearby alcove, a life-size figure of the great emancipator himself, seated in a Chippendale chair, surrounded by pictures and documents, mementoes of his successful campaign for the abolition of slavery.

In the same street is the classical fronted (1856) Corn Exchange, now housing the Museum of Transport and Archaeology, where evidence of man's inventive genius is displayed in items large and small familiar in the streets of yesterday. At the back, and shown under modern conditions of lighting and arrangement, the great Roman pavements from Rudston and Brantingham take you back to the culture of earlier dwellers of the East Riding. I found the Corn Exchange a much happier place than Wilberforce House.

Other old buildings in High Street and its immediate neighbourhood emphasise how this area is one of daytime use only. Consulates, ships' brokers, accountants, solicitors and merchants occupy the former great houses of the old city. At night they are de-peopled, and an uneasy silence settles on the streets. High Street almost backs on to the River Hull, with bonded warehouses occupying some of the intervening space.

Back into Market Place, which continues southwards as Queen Street as far as the river front where, at the junction of the River Hull with the Humber, Victoria Pier is the terminal of the car-ferry across the Humber to New Holland on the Lincolnshire bank. From here you can see the bigger ships gliding along the muddy waters. As third port in the country, handling annually cargoes to a Customs value of almost £1,000 million, the port of Hull has steadily increased its dock facilities which now extend for seven miles along the north bank of the river. Eight docks provide 12 miles of quays in addition to the two tidal riverside ones, and three deep-water oil jetties accept the large tankers. Closer links with Europe have benefited Hull as the major east coast port, and the roll on/roll off techniques are constantly in action. The King George Dock terminal handles some 200,000 passengers a year on the fast routes to Rotterdam and Zeebruggë, while the enormous fishing-trade is dealt with exclusively in St Andrew's Dock.

Hull Docks seem to be divorced from the main life of the city in much the same way as Old Town is. Drive along the streets towards the docks and you soon find the guarded gates and officialdom; drive eastwards towards the River Hull and you find the smell of dereliction and wasteland, although many of these empty spaces are planned to sprout huge new buildings – office blocks I suppose – and the noise of building work in Lowgate assaults the ears.

In fact noise is one of my persistent memories of Hull. Perhaps because so much of the East Riding is rural and peaceful, except at weekends, the roar of Hull seems so much greater. One-way street systems in the centre doubtless speed the traffic flow, but faster vehicles make more noise. Brick and concrete canyons capture it, reflect it, enfold it, so I found little pleasure in being a pedestrian in Queen Victoria Square, or in Alfred Gelder Street and Whitefriargate leading eastwards from it (with the Land of Green Ginger between them).

When Hull expanded in late Georgian times it did so in the area north of the square and of Queen's Gardens. George Street, Jarratt Street, and Albion Street are very much a shadow of their former elegance, partly through war damage, regrettably through demolition. One happy survival north of George Street is the Charterhouse, almshouses founded by Sir Michael de la Pole in 1384, but the present building of pale brown brick is 1778–80. Occupied by many elderly citizens of Hull, its upkeep comes from original endowments, whose value diminishes in the harsh economic climate of today, presenting continual worries for the Master and the hard-working Matron. Opposite it, in the garden of the Master's house, I found an oasis of quiet peace not far from the centre of the city, and was shown what purports to be the oldest living thing in Hull – a venerable mulberry tree which was thriving when Andrew Marvell's father was Master here early in the seventeenth century.

The shopping and business centre of Hull stretches along straight roads north and west from Queen Victoria Square. There are no gradients in central Hull, no subtleties of elevation changes, and precious few curves. Even the flower-beds bordering the pavement of Paragon Street have a rectangular rigidity. Many of the modern buildings are characteristically cuboid, although a number of worthwhile exceptions show façades of elegant brickwork, Georgian-style windows, classical columns and the occasional pediment. From the decade before the First World War, the City Hall and Guildhall dominate in the grand Edwardian Baroque manner of carved stone and deep cornice, while at the southern end of Paragon Street, G. T. Andrews' grandly classical Paragon Station of 1846 has much of his original Station Hotel adjoining it.

Hull has tried hard to compensate for the starkness of its situation. Plenty of flower-beds add their quotas of colour, but suburban garden-type displays invariably seem out of place, as though a guilty conscience is eased by a geometric planting of flowers. The addition of wooden seats emphasise the hostility of the surrounding elements. There are few, if any, pedestrian precincts, so that to escape the noise you appreciate the handy availability of the Ferens Art Gallery, with its good collection of paintings, particularly strong in modern British work, as well as Old Masters from Britain and the Netherlands.

One other thing is lacking from the streets of Hull, and its immediate neighbourhood. There are no red telephone kiosks, for the city is unique in the whole of Britain in having its own municipal telephone system, whose public call-boxes are painted cream. In 1904 Hull opened its first exchange, the result of a facility permitted by an Act of Parliament five years previously. The system serves the city and the surrounding district and is linked to the G.P.O. for trunk calls. It provides the normal type of telephone service and adds a number of local facilities such as a guide to entertainment.

Immediately beyond the busy shopping and commercial centre of Hull is the 'twilight zone' characteristic of so many cities' Victorian development; a gridiron pattern of now mean streets of brick terrace houses, corner pubs, dead shops with boarded windows. Whole areas are scheduled for development, but meanwhile the process of decay accelerates.

Spreading further outwards along the main roads from Hull, eastwards along Hedon Road to Marfleet, westward by Hessle Road or Anlaby Road, northwards by Spring Bank or Beverley Road, the greyness of the inner suburbs comes first, followed by the dreary similarities of post-war accretions. Eastwards are the docks, warehouses, old factories, new trading estates, the great Victorian prison, high walls, hoardings, and after a short green pause, Hedon. North-east, eventually is Sutton, which retains an identity of its own, and a particularly good church of early brick, mainly of the fourteenth century when it became collegiate and was consecrated.

A modern ring road arcs its way round the north of Hull. It may speed the traffic, but it also confirms the environmental mish-mash arising from so much piecemeal development. The road to Beverley is one of the most depressing in the East Riding, with no apparent end to roadside spoliation. Yet this is the road that leads to one of the loveliest of English towns, even if it does enter it by the gas-works. When, eventually, a few fields are reached the flatness of the countryside is merely a plain on which the armies of pylons do battle against the skyline.

Cottingham, in the north-west, is more of a small town than a village, with an identity, a history, and a market square. Its castle has long since gone, but parts of the moat are still iden-tifiable behind Northgate. Proudly dominating the centre of the town is the fine Perpendicular crossing tower of the parish church. Cottingham's Nonconformist Chapel of 1819 is one of the best in the East Riding, and there are a number of good houses of the eighteenth and nineteenth centuries which helped to boost its reputation of being the largest village in England.

Most of the Halls of Residence of Hull University are at Cot-tingham, the University buildings themselves being along the Cottingham road towards Hull. Founded in 1925, it did not acquire full University status until 1954, with the three faculties of arts, science, social sciences and law, in addition to a department of education. The extent of buildings on the cam-pus spans four decades of growth, from neo-Georgian brick, to modern cladding, yet it manages to keep a unity of its own, although it is not a patch on that of York.

We entered the East Riding at York, deep in history, proud in its past, splendid in its stones. We end it at Hull, a medieval town, a busy and bustling port with its eyes facing eastwards to Europe. The East Riding has ceased to exist as an administrative unit; most of it is embodied in the new Humberside, centred on Hull, where the great modern bridge will link Lincolnshire with Yorkshire not very far from where the Romans first crossed the Humber. Down the river the warning beacons wink at night all the way to Spurn where the great river meets the restless sea.

INDEX

Index

Index

Landscape,
  General, 13, 14–16
  Holderness, 10, 56, 70, 74
  Wolds, 10, 86, 102, 110–11, 121,
    122–3, 139
Langtoft, 119
Langton, 16, 165
Lawrence, T. E. (of Arabia), 52, 109
Laxton, 178
Leavening, 111, 112
Leconfield, 154
Leven, 82
  Canal, 82–3
Lightoller, Thomas, 78, 79
Little Denmark, see Flamborough
Little Weighton, 137
Lockington, 154–5
Londesborough, Alfred Denison, 1st Earl
  of, 127
Londesborough, 12, 19, 126–7
Lowthorpe, 93
Lund, 157

Malton, 61, 164, 174, 175
Market Weighton, 135–6
  Canal, 175, 179
Marvell, Andrew, 19, 74, 185
Meaux Abbey, 13, 59, 81–2, 181
Melbourne, 131
Middleton-on-the-Wolds, 124
Millington, 14, 122
  Pastures, 122–3
Monasteries, 13, 23, 24–5, 49–50, 58, 59,
  80–2, 127–8, 155–6, 165–6, 169, 172,
  174, 181
  Dissolution of, 13, 25, 49
Moore, Temple, 12, 74, 83, 94 106, 116,
  122, 128
Morris, Rev. Francis Orpen, 128
Motorway, 19, 178, 181

Naburn, 172
Nafferton, 97–8
Nature Reserves,
  Bempton Cliffs, 43–4, 54
  Hornsea Mere, 59
  Skipwith Common, 169
  Spurn, 66
  Wharram Quarry, 115
  Wheldrake Ings, 169
Navigations, see Canals
Neolithic Age, 11
New Earswick, 33
Newport, 178–9
Normans, 12–13, 23, 56
North Burton, 118
North Cave, 139
North Dalton, 124
North Ferriby, 180
North Frodingham, 83
North Grimston, 112

North Landing, 45, 47
North Newbald, 12, 137
North Sea Gas, 57–8, 65
Norton, 164
Nunburnholme, 12, 13, 127–8, 72
Nunkeeling, 13

Open fields, 13, 110, 115, 123, 127, 134
Ottringham, 75
Ouse River, 9, 11, 13, 26

Painsthorpe, 111
Patrington, 12, 69–70, 73
Paulinus, 12, 23, 38, 126, 131
Paull, 77
  Holme Tower, 13, 77
Pavements, Roman, 91–2
Pearson, J. L., 12, 60, 102, 122, 132, 134,
  154, 157, 172, 180
Pearson, Capt. Sir Richard, R.N., 48
Percy family, 128–9, 154, 173
Pevsner, Sir Nikolaus, 69, 102, 109, 132,
  143, 153
Pickering, Lake, 13, 162
  Vale of, 10
Pilgrimage of Grace, 13, 50, 173
Pocklington, 20, 129–30
  Canal, 16, 129, 130–1
Preston, 77

Raikes Mausoleum, 144
Railways, 16, 27, 77, 97, 100, 101, 110,
  114, 124, 129, 130, 136, 175
Raisthorpe, 113
Ramblers' Association, 123
Ravenser, 68, 77
Ravenserodd, 68
Reclamation, 10, 70, 73–4
Reighton, 42
Riccall, 170
Rillington, 164
Roads, 11, 105, 111
  Roman, 111, 126, 136, 180
  Turnpike, 14, 135
Romans, 11, 21–3, 24, 28, 91–2, 112, 119,
  126, 136, 180
Roos, 61–2
Rose, Joseph, 104
Rowley, 137–8
Rowntree, Seebohm, 19, 33
Royal Society for Protection of Birds, 43,
  59
Rudston, 86–8, 91–2
  Standing stone, 11, 86–7

Saltmarshe Hall, 178
Salvin, A, 112
Sancton, 137
Saxons, 11, 23
Scagglethorpe, 164
Scampston Hall, 163